PRAISES FOR AMERICAN ST. NICK

"One more memorable and inspiring story from the greatest generation—soldiers who put down their weapons and brought Christmas to a beleaguered town and its kids. It will touch your heart and make you proud."

—*Tom Brokaw*

"On December 5, 1944, against the bleak backdrop of World War II, a group of American GIs unleashed the strongest weapon in their arsenal: humanity. Peter Lion recaptures the magic of Santa to transcend even the darkest of times. The children of Wiltz, Luxembourg, never forgot their American St. Nick. And now neither will you."

—*Meredith Vieira, coanchor of NBC's* Today *(2006–2011),*
TV talk show host, journalist

"Better than any Christmas fable, this is a remarkable true story that I can't believe I didn't know: American soldiers putting down their guns in the heat of World War II battle to offer a sliver of light and holiday hope. An uplifting must-read."

—*Willie Geist, coanchor of NBC's* Today *and MSNBC's* Morning Joe

"Richard Brookings is a real-live American legend who is honored every single year in Wiltz on December 6. His story and how it affected Luxembourgers during the war is touching and should be heard by all."

—*Alison Shorter-Lawrence, Chargé d'Affaires, US Embassy Luxembourg*

The day American soldiers brought Christmas back to one
Luxembourg town during the darkest days of WWII

AMERICAN ST. NICK

A TRUE STORY

PETER LION

Plain Sight Publishing
An imprint of Cedar Fort, Inc. • Springville, UT

ISBN 13: 978-1-4621-1762-8

Published by Plain Sight Publishing, an imprint of Cedar Fort, Inc.
2373 W. 700 S., Springville, UT 84663
Distributed by Cedar Fort, Inc., www.cedarfort.com

LIBRARY OF CONGRESS CATALOGING-IN-PUBLICATION DATA

Lion, Peter, author.
American St. Nick : a true story / Peter Lion.
pages cm
Includes bibliographical references.
ISBN 978-1-4621-1762-8 (perfect bound : alk. paper)
1. United States. Army. Infantry Division, 28th. Signal Company, 28th. 2. Brookins, Richard. 3. Wiltz (Luxembourg)--History--20th century. 4. Saint Nicolas' Day--Luxembourg--Wiltz--History. I. Title. II. Title: American Saint Nick.
D769.36328th .L562 2015
394.2663094935--dc23
                2015022013

Cover design by Lauren Error
Cover design © 2015 by Lyle Mortimer
Edited and typeset by Eileen Leavitt

Printed in the United States of America

10 9 8 7 6 5 4 3 2 1

Printed on acid-free paper

To the members of the 28th Infantry Division: ROLL ON!
To the people of Wiltz for always remembering.
And to you, for wanting to know the story.

"IF LUXEMBOURG WOULD STAND ANOTHER THOUSAND YEARS,
WE WILL ALWAYS BE GRATEFUL TO THE AMERICAN SOLDIERS
AND THEIR MOST BRAVE AND VALIANT NATION, WHO GAVE
THEIR BLOOD SO THAT WE MAY LIVE IN A FREE EUROPE."

—FATHER VICTOR WOLFF (1977)

CONTENTS

CHAPTER 1: 1977 1

CHAPTER 2 7

CHAPTER 3 15

CHAPTER 4: 1944 23

CHAPTER 5 29

CHAPTER 6 41

CHAPTER 7 51

CHAPTER 8 59

CHAPTER 9 71

CHAPTER 10 79

CHAPTER 11: 1977 105

CHAPTER 12 115

CHAPTER 13 121

CHAPTER 14 131

OF NOTE 135

ABOUT THE AUTHOR 149

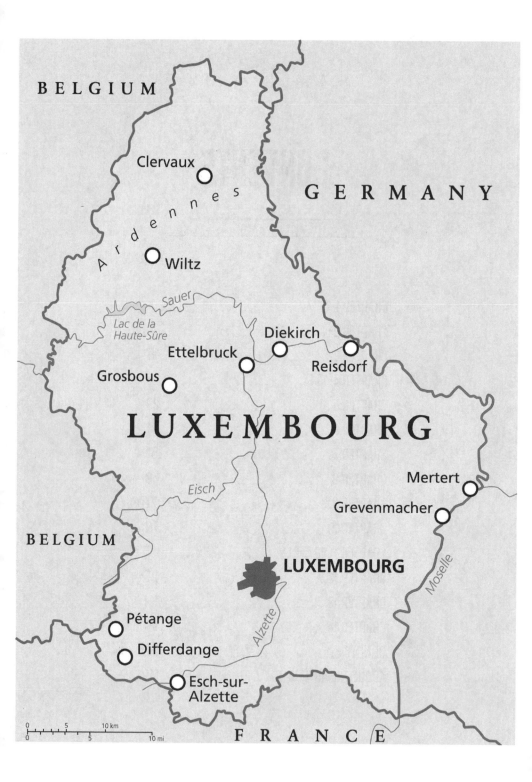

CHAPTER 1

1977

"It's amazing we weren't all killed," he mumbled through a heavy sigh. Through a light rain falling since morning but now easing as the afternoon waned, he surveyed the dense forest surrounding him and was surprised by how little it had changed. The forest floor, with only hints of sunlight on the brightest of days, was littered with pine needles, wispy ferns, and the dead branches of ancient pines stretching skyward ninety feet or more—standing testaments to the creep of time in these woods that Frank McClelland had come to visit on the outskirts of Doncols, Luxembourg. He came here to remember, certainly, but also to forget. He came with the hope of finding the answer to a question that had remained stored but never really forgotten in a corner of his mind for more than thirty years.

He was a solid-framed man, his sixty-two years marked not by his barrel-chested build but rather by thinning black hair mixed with threads of white and by a rounded, pugnacious face; a pair of rectangular, gold-colored wire-rimmed glasses perched at the notch on his nose. As the distance between now and the then of the war grew, Frank wondered what, if anything, could he have done differently back on that bitterly cold snowy December day in 1944. It was a painful question he repeated to himself through the years as time tried to heal his emotional and physical wounds. Frank knew he would never find his answer without going *there*, being *there*, and standing in *those* woods once again. He knew that if he could return to this stand of trees in this patch of woods, it would somehow take him back in time, slicing through the layers of years to

December 21, 1944, when twenty-nine-year-old Sergeant Frank McClelland led a small group of MPs and soldiers out of the town of Wiltz for the last time.

The MPs had been the last of the rear guard of the American 28th Infantry Division ordered to hold the town as long as possible against the attacking Germans, buying time for the rest of the soldiers to withdraw. Once the town was clear, Frank and his men were to move along any of the available roads snaking through the Ardennes ahead of the swiftly advancing Germans and get to the town of Bastogne in Belgium a few dozen miles to the west.

It was the beginning of the last major German offensive of World War II—an offensive that Army Command had deemed highly unlikely. The German Army was said to be on the defensive, retreating into Germany and fortifying its defenses for a final stand against an Allied push. The fall of Berlin and the end of the war were forthcoming. There was a chance that the war might even be over by Christmas but certainly by the New Year.

What command hadn't told them was Army Intelligence had information to the contrary—information indicating that the Germans were amassing troops in the Ardennes. The commanders at division headquarters had also ignored information from townspeople living near the front lines. Local people had been detained, questioned by the Germans, and then released. They had risked their lives to tell the Americans what they had witnessed—the buildup of German troops, armor and artillery—but the information was set aside.

It was here in these Luxembourg hills, along a front thinly protected by American troops, that the Germans launched a surprise counterattack and pushed through the American lines in an effort to reach Antwerp, thus driving a wedge between the Allied forces. The Battle of the Bulge had begun. In the six weeks of fighting that followed, more than a million men would engage in battle along an eighty-mile-long and fifty-mile-wide front line. It would prove to be the largest and bloodiest battle of the war, with the Americans suffering 89,000 casualties including 19,000 soldiers killed and more than 47,500 wounded. German losses were even greater, with an estimated 100,000 men killed, missing, or wounded. Additionally, more than three thousand civilians were killed, some executed by German soldiers for aiding the Americans. As the fighting raged, scores of towns were turned to rubble.

In Wiltz, the 28th Division headquarters was overrun by the German spearhead. In some of the fiercest fighting of the war, Frank and the other MPs, along with a handful of soldiers who volunteered to stay behind, held the town until the morning of December 20. When it was finally cleared of troops and any civilians who wanted to leave with the American troops, Sergeant McClelland and his men assembled behind a light armor tank and followed it out of Wiltz ahead of the German assault.

They had gone only about a mile toward Bastogne when they were spotted by a group of German infantry. The Germans quickly opened fire, disabling the small tank with a rocket from a Panzerfaust antitank gun. Machine gun and small arms fire followed, and Frank and the others were forced to scatter and retreat into the thickly wooded hills.

For the remainder of the day and into the night, the men managed to dodge German troops by moving carefully and quietly through the woods. Heavy snowfall and blankets of thick fog slowed their progress but also provided some extra cover. The following day, however, that same snow and fog that had helped hide the MPs now caused them to walk right by a squad of German soldiers. The weather conditions had concealed the Germans so well that Frank and his men didn't see or hear them until they yelled and opened fire.

The peaceful forest erupted. Frank and his men instinctively dove to the ground for cover. Bullets ripped the air, splintered trees, and threw up tufts of mud and snow. Then as the shooting abruptly stopped, Frank could hear someone yelling in German. He cautiously lifted his head and spied several German soldiers approaching through the smoke and trees. The Germans were yelling commands as they slowly advanced, their weapons trained on the MPs. Although he understood only a few words and phrases in German, Frank knew he and his men were being told to surrender. He looked around to check on the other men. Most only looked scared and confused, but two of them weren't moving, the snow around them melting and mottled a reddish-brown. Frank again looked up at the advancing Germans, their weapons ready to tear into the Americans. Their situation hopeless, Frank put his head down and breathed deeply, taking in the scent of fresh snow, wet earth, and cordite. He slowly rose to his knees, tossing his Thompson submachine gun to the side and cautiously raising his arms, all the while holding his breath. He said nothing as he surrendered. His men looked at each other for a few moments, and then reluctantly mimicked his actions.

For the rest of the day, the men—now POWs—were marched east through the Luxembourg countryside and deeper into once again German-held territory. They had no food and little water and ate snow to keep up their strength. By nightfall the cold, hungry, thirsty, and exhausted soldiers were taken to a barn just outside the small farming community of Nocher. After having them sit in the barn for several hours, the Germans began interrogating the soldiers, trying to glean any information they could about Allied troops' movements and strengths. The interrogations started with Frank. He stood while they fired question after question at him, but he repeatedly offered only name, rank, and serial number. Even when the German captain leading the interrogation delivered backhand blows to Frank's face and head, he repeated only his name, rank, and serial number.

The captain's frustrations grew until finally he pulled his pistol from its holster and barked out commands. Three German soldiers grabbed Frank and pulled him outside the barn, the captain still yelling. Frank didn't understand the German officer, but as he was hurried along, he suddenly realized what was happening. He was about to be executed. Stepping out into the cold, snowy night, one of the German soldiers, the oldest looking of the trio, whispered to Frank in broken English, "No shoot." Frank was scared and now stunned. The German's grizzled, battle-soiled face showing a reassuring countenance. Frank's fear quickly abated, along with the knot in his stomach. It was all a ruse designed to entice the other POWs to talk. None did.

Frank would spend the next two months as a prisoner of war. He was moved to three different POW camps in Europe, and then finally to a camp in Poland. By that time, the German army was back on the defensive. Their advance through Europe had been halted by the heroics and tenacity of the Allied forces. Frank's POW camp was eventually liberated by the Russian army as it advanced on the Germans from the east.

For Frank, the war was just about over, but in those two months as a POW and in the tormented nightmare-filled years that followed, one question lingered—what, if anything, could he have done differently to prevent his capture and the deaths of two of his men?

Now, after returning to this forest, Frank realized that nothing would have changed the events of that day. He and his men had been unlucky—plain and simple. Despite all their training and caution, the woods had been too overgrown, the fog too thick, the snow too heavy, and the Germans wearing white battle dress too well concealed. There was no way he or his men could have avoided them.

After more than thirty years, Frank finally had his answer. He took a deep breath, the moist evening air filling his lungs. He saw everything differently now. Everything in his memory was clearer. He scanned his surroundings once again. "It's a wonder we made it this far."

He stood with hands fisted, buried deep in his jacket pockets. Sunlight now strained against the steel-gray clouds. He took a deep breath and slowly, deliberately, gave the wooded hillside a final look. As he peered through the trees, he could feel his eyes begin to swell with tears. He looked down for a few moments and thought about the war and, in particular, the friends who never made it out of these woods. "Such a waste," he whispered.

He cleared his throat. Another deep breath and then he turned and headed back to the car. He hiked the few hundred yards back to the rain-wet logging road—one of many that now weaved through the forest. As he left the tree line, he spotted his navy-blue rental car parked along the edge of the road, just as he'd left it hours earlier. He didn't have a planned itinerary, but he knew where he wanted to go and what he wanted to see while retracing his steps from three decades ago. Eventually, he would have to drive to the airport in Frankfort for the trip home, but for now, he had the entire week to relive the war, and that was fine with him. Tomorrow he would drive into Germany to the site of the first camp where he had been held prisoner. But tonight he'd head to Wiltz. As far as he was concerned, his POW ordeal had begun there when he and his men were ordered to hold the town. Besides, Wiltz was the closest town where he knew he'd be able to find a hotel for the night.

He squeezed back into the small European car, and then chuckled at his absentmindedness. He'd left the keys dangling from the ignition on the dashboard, but at least he hadn't locked himself out of the car. He started the engine, carefully maneuvered the car around on the dirt road, and headed east. A few minutes later, he rounded a bend and saw the sign reading, "WILTZ 6km."

CHAPTER 2

The storybook town of Wiltz is a picturesque vacation retreat nestled in the forested hills of northern Luxembourg. Most of the town had been damaged by friendly fire when the Americans were forced to retake it from the Germans during the Battle of the Bulge, but under the Marshall Plan, the town eventually rebuilt, and to Frank's astonishment as he drove down the Rue de la Fontaine, the Hotel Bellevue was still there.

Frank remembered it well. After the Americans liberated Luxembourg, the town of Wiltz had become the headquarters for the 28th Infantry Division, and the Hotel Bellevue had been used to billet soldiers, with the bottom floor converted into a mess hall. Frank also remembered how the people of the town had celebrated when the American army liberated them and how they had opened their homes to the GIs. But Frank also remembered the feelings of shame, guilt, and confusion when the Americans were forced to pull out of Wiltz, once again leaving the town and its people in the hands of the Germans, especially the feared and hated SS.

Frank drove slowly past the hotel and allowed the waves of memories to wash over him. He pulled the car to the side of the road just past the hotel, parked, and retrieved his bag from the trunk. He entered the hotel and was greeted by a broad smile from the woman behind the small reception desk.

Before she could speak, Frank blurted out, "Hello," hoping that she understood English. He'd picked up a bit of German during the war, but with no opportunity to speak it since, he knew it would be choppy at best, and getting a room for the night might prove difficult.

"Hello. What may I do for you?" the woman asked.

A sense of relief washed over Frank. "I was hoping to get a room for the night. Just one night. I'll be leaving in the morning."

The woman looked to be in her sixties, Rubenesque, with long, meticulously braided gray hair. "Just one night then?" she asked, with a hint of a British accent.

"Yes, please. Do you have any rooms available?"

"Certainly," the woman smiled as she handed Frank a registration card and then looked for a room key in the mail slots on the wall behind her.

"I was wondering, is the restaurant still open?" Frank asked, nodding at the small hotel restaurant and bar in the adjacent room—the one he'd noticed through the window overlooking the street on the way in. "I was hoping to get something to eat. I've been traveling all day."

"The restaurant? Yes, of course."

She handed him keys to a room and pointed the way to the stairs as he picked up his suitcase.

"Room twenty-four. Do you need help with your luggage?" she asked, although she noticed that Frank had just one bag.

"No, no. I think I can manage," Frank said, smiling. As he climbed the narrow stairs to the third floor, he wondered who would have carried his bag to the room had he replied with a yes. No doubt she would have, and he would have none of that.

When he got to his room, Frank threw the suitcase on the bed, unlatched it, and removed a shaving kit from the neatly packed contents. *If there's one thing the army teaches you*, he thought, *it's how to pack and travel light*. He carried the shaving kit into the small bathroom, turned on the water, and washed his hands. Then he repeatedly splashed the cool tap water onto his face. He dried his hands and face, and feeling refreshed, went back downstairs to the hotel dining room.

He stood in the doorway of the restaurant for a moment, surveying the small room. Through a thin pall of cigarette smoke, Frank eyed a small but ornately carved black oak bar running along the length of the wall to his right, leaving just enough space in the room for half a dozen small round tables and a larger table against the window overlooking the street.

Aside from two men sitting at the far end of the bar away from the door, Frank was the only person in the room. The two men nodded slightly at the stranger—a foreigner in their bar. Frank returned the nod as the woman from the reception desk reappeared from behind a curtain at end of the room and motioned to Frank for him to sit down. She placed a one-page trilingual menu in front of him.

"Would you like something to drink? Some wine or beer perhaps?" the woman asked, turning her shoulders slightly towards the ornately carved bar.

"I'd love a beer. One of the local beers, if possible," Frank answered, and then, thinking that she might not understand the word *local*, he added, "I mean one that's made here . . . in Luxembourg."

"Yes, of course," she said, smiling as she turned and walked to the bar. She placed a stein, something for the tourists of course, under the spigot and pulled down on the tap handle to fill the large, oversized mug.

"We have some of the best beers in Luxembourg made right here in Wiltz," she announced proudly on her return, placing the brimming mug on the table.

"Is that so?"

"Yes. Simon Pils. You have heard of it, yes? There is a brewery right here in Wiltz," she said, casting a look towards the front of the room at the window overlooking the street and to somewhere beyond. "In the castle," she added.

"Oh, yes," Frank suddenly recalled. He raised the mug to his lips and sipped. "Better than I remember," he said as he licked the foam from his top lip. "Very good!"

The woman smiled in appreciation. She took his dinner order, smiled once again, and disappeared behind the curtain.

Frank sipped the golden beer while drinking in the details of the dining room. He remembered the room looking much different than the last time he was here, but that was during the war; everything looked different then. At that time, it was a room with long tables and benches— GIs huddled over mess kits eating overly salted, reconstituted whatever the company cooks could pull together in the field kitchen across the street. At least the coffee was good; hot and strong, or at least that's how Frank remembered it.

It wasn't long before the woman returned with a plate and some bread.

"Your dinner should be ready soon," she told Frank, and then after a slight pause, she asked, "You are on holiday, yes?"

"Yes. I'm traveling all over. That is, I'm here in Luxembourg today, but I'm planning to head into Germany tomorrow."

"I see," the woman said, as she smiled and nodded, "You are English?"

"English?" Frank laughed with surprise. "No, I'm an American. I was here during the war," he explained in his deep, scratchy voice—the kind that oozed authority and confidence.

"Oh, I see. Then perhaps you were with the American 28th Army?" the woman replied, curiosity unmistakable in her tone.

"Yes," Frank answered, this time even more surprised. "I was an MP—that's military police—assigned to the 28th *Division.*" He emphasized the word in an effort to politely correct her mistake.

"Yes, yes. *Division*, of course," she smiled. "Then you were here, at the hotel before, yes? This is my hotel. My husband and I—I was here then, during the war."

Frank looked closely at the woman, trying to peel away the layered years to recall her face.

"I remember this hotel all right," Frank recalled. "I was here all the time. It's where we had our mess hall—our dining area," he explained. "I know some of the guys were billeted—they stayed here—but I wasn't one of them. I was in a house up the street." Another swallow of beer. "I used to walk by here all the time. Headquarters was just down the road around the corner if I remember correctly. A big house."

"Yes, that is correct. It is now the home of a chemist—that is—how does one say?" she paused, searching. "Pharmacist," she blurted out, pleased at her success. "Their family—Martzen is their name. Mr. Pierre Martzen. Our name is Rasquin, Marie Rasquin."

"McClelland," Frank responded slowly and clearly. "Frank McClelland."

"Yes, I remember."

"You do?" Frank was amazed and more than a little skeptical that she had remembered him from more than thirty years earlier.

"Of course. From earlier—the front desk," she giggled.

"Oh, yes," Frank laughed off his embarrassment.

"I am sorry, but I do not remember you from the war," Marie apologized. "It was so long ago. So many soldiers. You understand."

"Yes, I do understand. I must say, the hotel looks wonderful. Better than the last time I saw it."

"Well, I should hope so; it was quite a long time ago. We have had time rebuild. To change things," she said lightheartedly and then disappeared behind the curtain for a few minutes. Something in her tone however hinted at more to her story.

In fact, during the war, Marie Rasquin had to manage running the hotel and raising her family on her own. Her husband, Nicolas, had been taken prisoner by the Germans, and Marie did not see him again until the war ended. When the horror of war came to Wiltz during the Battle of the Bulge, Marie huddled in the basement of the hotel with her three children and other family members and friends for nearly six weeks, hoping and praying Allied bombs wouldn't fall on the hotel. Her prayers were heard, and by the end of January, the Germans were once again forced out of Wiltz, and she and her family came out of hiding to a heavily damaged but still-standing hotel and home.

"Is there anything else you need?" Marie asked reentering the room and placing a dinner plate in front of Frank.

"Not right now. I think I'm all set."

"Perhaps another beer?" she offered.

"Sure, why not? This I do remember. It's what we drank; it's all we had. Tastes better now; but then again, that was a long time ago." Frank poured the remainder of the beer into his mouth.

As Marie moved behind the bar and began pouring another beer, Frank noticed her talking to the two men seated there, while nodding in Frank's direction. She returned to the table and placed the beer in front of him, removed the empty mug.

"Excuse me, but I was wondering: since you were with the 28th Division, would you mind meeting some men from Wiltz?" She asked, motioning at the two men seated at the bar. "They would very much like to meet you. But after you have finished eating, of course."

"Sure. Okay, why not? But why do they want to talk to me?"

"They always want to meet soldiers from the 28th Division."

"Okay, I guess," Frank agreed. "But why wait? I'll talk to them now if they want."

She thanked him and walked over to the men at the bar. Frank couldn't hear what they were saying. After a few moments of conversation, the two men looked over at him and smiled courteously as they rose to follow Marie back to Frank's table.

"This is Mr. McClelland," Marie announced to the men. She then retreated to the kitchen, leaving the three to talk.

Frank tried to stand up to greet the men, but one of them was politely waving him down.

"Please, do not get up," the man said in heavily accented English as he extended his hand. Of medium build with a thin, lined face and sporting a wide smile, he had shoe-polish black hair graying slightly at the temples and looked to be about fifty years old. "My name is Jeanly Schweig, and this is Raymond Braas. Good evening."

"Good evening," Frank answered cheerfully.

"Marie said you were an American soldier, and you were here in Wiltz, during the war."

"Yes, that's right."

"You were with the American 28th Division?" asked Raymond, the heavier and older looking of the two, with deep-set eyes hidden behind thickly framed glasses.

"Yes. I was an MP back then. In fact, I was captured by the Germans just outside of Wiltz, near Doncols."

"Ah, yes. Doncols," Raymond replied, pronouncing the name correctly.

"Will you be staying here in Wiltz long?" asked Jeanly.

"Well, no," Frank began sheepishly, hoping not to offend the two men, "I was planning to head out tomorrow."

"I see," said Jeanly. "I know you must have plans, but it would be an honor if you would stop by our museum for a tour."

"Museum? I didn't know there was a museum here in town."

"Yes, it's at the castle, our museum. Raymond is the . . . ," Jeanly paused as he searched for the right word in English. He turned to Raymond and muttered something Frank didn't understand. Raymond shrugged. "How do you say it—he is in charge."

"Oh, *the curator?*" Frank offered.

"Yes. That is it. Raymond is the curator of the museum."

"It is to honor the soldiers of the Battle of the Bulge who fought here for us during the war—and especially the American 28th Division," Raymond explained. "The museum is in the castle—the Wiltz castle. It would be a great honor if you could come and see it."

Frank could see the pride the two men had for their museum, and he didn't want to disappoint them. Plus, they had piqued his curiosity, and now he wanted to see for himself just what would be on display in a war museum in a town this small. Most of Europe was dotted with monuments and museums dedicated to the war, but this was the first time he'd ever heard of a museum devoted almost entirely to a single unit—his unit.

"Well, why not? I'd love to," he finally agreed.

"Wonderful," Schweig exclaimed. "When will you be there?"

"I want to head over to Germany tomorrow, but I could come by first thing in the morning, if that's all right."

"Yes, we will be there. Is ten o'clock in the morning a good time?" Raymond asked.

"Sure, that'll be fine," Frank said.

Just then, Marie emerged from behind the curtain. From across the room, she spoke to the two men in what sounded like German, and then in English she added, "That is enough. Let him eat in peace now." Jeanly and Raymond waved off her scolds and turned back to Frank.

"Marie . . . she is a wonderful cook. The best in Wiltz," Jeanly smiled. "Enjoy your dinner. Tomorrow we will see you at the castle at ten." The three men shook hands, and Jeanly and Raymond retreated back to the bar.

As Frank began eating, he couldn't help thinking about the museum. The more he thought about it, the more it interested him. He knew the American army was well regarded by the people of Wiltz, and the rest of the country for that matter. This was evident from the American flag raised alongside the Luxembourg flag at the American Military Cemetery in Hamm and at other war memorials he'd visited on his way here. But a museum dedicated to the 28th—now that was intriguing. Frank smiled to himself. He was glad the men had asked him to visit the museum. It would delay his trip into Germany by a few hours at most, and now that he knew about the museum, he wouldn't have missed it for the world.

CHAPTER 3

The castle of Wiltz sits majestically in the lush forest on the northern end of town, resembling more a sprawling French château than
a medieval European castle. Construction first began in the thirteenth
century, but the castle was twice destroyed by fire: once in 1388, when
French invaders burned the town to the ground, and again in 1453, when
Philip of Burgundy attacked the manor. Each time, the castle was rebuilt,
but wars, sieges, famines, and plagues often delayed construction. The
castle was finally completed in 1720. Then, during the French revolution,
it was confiscated, declared national property, and sold at public auction.
The castle remained in private hands for more than a century until 1951,
when it was bought and renovated by the Luxembourg state. During
World War II, the castle served as a convent and girls' boarding school
run by the Nuns of the Christian Doctrine. Allied bombs destroyed parts
of the castle in the fighting to retake Wiltz during the Battle of the Bulge,
and once again, the castle was rebuilt. Today it houses a retirement home,
a tourist office, the Simon Pils brewery and museum, as well as a museum
dedicated to the Battle of the Bulge. Plus, each year in the large amphitheater adjacent to the courtyard, the Wiltz Festival plays host to a series
of outdoor performances ranging from jazz and classical music concerts
to operas.

Following a light breakfast in the same room where he'd had dinner
the night before, Frank checked out of the hotel, walked down Rue de
la Fontaine and onto the Grand Rue. He passed by numerous shops and
cafés, the town's florist located directly across from town hall, around

the front of the Hotel Vieux Château at the bend in the Grand Rue, and finally up the cobbled entrance to the castle.

The castle looked much the same as when he last saw it in 1944, although it was obvious that it had undergone renovations and updates. After stopping to take a few pictures of the castle and the surrounding countryside, Frank went to a doorway to the left of the portico: the main entrance to the castle museum. Jeanly and Raymond were already there to greet him, and the trio began to talk about the war and the town in general as they made their way through the small museum.

A series of glass cases and displays held artifacts from the war. Among them were mannequins clad in both German and American uniforms, various personal items donated by individual soldiers, and standard issue equipment that any soldier might have carried—mess kits, canteens, and even K rations. There were also various weapons from both armies. Guns, bullets, mortar shells, grenades, and land mines (all rendered harmless) now lay as grim reminders of the past. And there were pictures—scores and scores of pictures lining the walls.

As the men walked through the museum, Frank stopped several times, intently looking, almost staring at the relics and pictures. A flood of memories for which he was ill-prepared washed over him.

At one of the displays, Frank stopped and gazed at a German machine gun.

"That's the one," he muttered, pointing at the rusted weapon. "Obviously not *that* one, but one just like it," he corrected.

"A German MP-40," Frank began, his eyes still trained on the weapon. "We used to call them 'burp guns,' and that's what we ran into the day I was captured. Do you remember last night when I said that I was captured near Doncols? Well, the way I remember it, it was pretty early in the morning, and it was cold. Coldest I've ever felt then or now. At least I seem to remember it like that. And snowing. It'd been snowing heavily off and on for most of the night, I think. Anyway, we were scattered all over the place, and we didn't know where anyone else from the division was. It was just a mess. Complete chaos. Well my squad—my guys and the stragglers we picked up along the way—we were moving to the north or really northwest. We were trying to get to Bastogne. That was our plan anyway. That was supposed to be the rally point.

"We'd left Wiltz the day before, and we were moving through the woods near Doncols. I remember being cold and hungry, and we were still a long way from where we needed to be." Frank paused long enough to run a finger under his nose and clear his throat. "I remember us running into Germans all night. They were everywhere—or at least it sure seemed that way to us. We didn't even try to fight 'em or nothing since we were outmanned. We just kept moving trying to avoid 'em. But these guys—all of a sudden they opened up on us with this thing. It happened so fast, and yet to me it seemed like everything was in slow motion. Still does."

Frank paused for a few moments as his memories and emotions surged. Jeanly and Raymond said nothing, knowing that Frank still had more to say and realizing that anything they could add at this moment might sound trite.

"I'm sorry," Frank finally said, his voice cracking slightly. "Sometimes it's not easy remembering." Jeanly and Raymond nodded. Frank cleared his throat, took a deep breath, and continued.

"I can see it all clear as day. One of my guys—Jenkins. Nice guy. Just a kid really. From Indiana—he was on point, that is he was in the lead walking just a little ahead of me maybe ten or fifteen yards or so when they opened up on. He was hit right away in the face. It was like his head just . . . ," Frank stopped and looked up at the ceiling for a moment, the memories so clear it made him shudder. Gaining his composure, he continued. "I guess it was instinct or training or whatever you want to call it, but I dove into the snow. The funny thing is, I don't even remember doing it. I just remember looking up and seeing the Germans walking towards us, pointing their guns at us and yelling." Frank paused again, took a deep breath, and checked on the ceiling; it was still there. "Anyway, I lost Jenkins and another one of the guys, and the rest of us, well, we were all taken prisoner."

Frank was biting down on his lip, his eyes welling up. After a few moments, he looked over at Jeanly and Raymond and smiled tightly. Then he looked back at the gun in the display case. "Anyway. This was the type of gun they carried."

Jeanly and Raymond said nothing. They had understood every word.

"Come," said Jeanly softly. "There are some photographs over here."

The three men walked over to a group of simple black-framed photographs neatly arranged on the wall amid time-yellowed newspaper clippings under glass. In each of the half-dozen or so black–and–white photos, there was a common subject: a tall man with a long white beard, a priest maybe, on his way to church. The man was wearing white robes that trailed behind him, and on his head he wore a bishop's miter. In his left hand, he carried what looked like a shepherd's staff, and walking behind him were two little girls wearing white robes and what looked like angels' wings. In one picture, the three were riding in a US Army Jeep. Another photo showed the man walking through a part of town with another priest—this one dressed in black. In a third picture, the group appeared to be approaching a crowd of small children who had gathered with their parents. Just in front of the children, an American soldier playing a guitar.

Frank scanned the photographs curiously for several moments.

"Do you know this man?" Schweig asked pointing to the tall man in white robes.

"The priest?" asked Frank.

"No, no. He is not a priest," Jeanly stressed, pointing at the photograph. "This man, the one in the white, do you know *him*?"

"You're telling me he's not a priest?"

"No, not at all," Raymond said. "He is a soldier. An American soldier like you. That is, he was from the 28th."

"A soldier?" Frank asked with disbelief. "A GI? Really? You're kidding me."

"No, he is an American soldier from the 28th Division from the war. Of course, he is in costume in the photograph," Raymond explained.

"Oh, I see," Frank said tilting his head back as he studied the figures more carefully through the bottom half of his glasses. "No, I'm sorry, but I don't recognize him. It's a bit tough, what with the costume and all."

"But he is from the 28th, and you—you were in the 28th also, yes?"

Jeanly's tone suggested that Frank should know the man, so once again, Frank squinted at the old, grainy photographs and tried to recognize the soldier in white robes.

"It's tough to say," Frank finally conceded. "With all that stuff he's got on, I really can't make out the face, and you have to remember that there were a lot of GIs in the division. Somewhere in the neighborhood of six thousand."

"Well, this man is Richard Brookins. He is from Rochester in New York." Raymond said, pronouncing it as *row-shes-tay*. As he spoke, he handed Frank an old copy of a *Stars & Stripes* newspaper that Frank only now realized Raymond had carried neatly tucked under his arm the whole time. There on the front page was a copy of the same photo on the wall and the headline,

Private Brookins of Rochester Plays Saint Nicolas for the Children of Wiltz.

"Oh, okay," Frank said as he looked at the photo in the paper and then compared it to the one on the wall. He reread the caption above the picture, hoping the name would spark a memory.

"No, I'm sorry. I don't know him. This was such a long time ago."

"Of course, but he was in your division," Jeanly repeated and then pointedly asked, "Can you help us find him?"

"Find him?" Frank exclaimed, looking up from the tattered newspaper, "What do you mean 'find him'?"

"Yes. You were in the 28th. You must help us to find him—to locate him," Jeanly insisted.

"But . . . ," Frank's voice trailed off, his mind racing, "but that was more than thirty years ago. How can I find him now? He might not have even made it out of the war. I mean, he could be dead for all we know."

"When you go back to America, if he is alive, I know you will find him. Will you help us?" Jeanly pleaded persuasively.

"No, you don't understand. This guy might not have even survived the war," Frank repeated, overwhelmed at the idea of finding someone based on a thirty-year-old newspaper picture. "Even if he did make it, how am I supposed to go about finding him?"

"If he is alive, you will find him. I know you will," said Jeanly with an almost infectious confidence and smile. Frank stared at the picture, his thoughts churning. Even if this guy was alive, how was he going to find him? Where would he begin looking? Would this Brookins guy still be living in the same town after thirty years? Frank looked back at the two men; a "why me" expression plastered across his face.

"So why don't *you* guys try to find him? Can't you call the embassy or the army or something?"

"Yes, yes, we have tried, but they have found nothing, so we think. We have not heard from them," admitted Raymond.

"Well, if the embassy or the army couldn't help, what makes you think I'm going to do any better? I mean I'm sure they have records at their disposal."

What none of them knew was that four years earlier, just after

midnight on July 12, 1973, a fire erupted at the National Archives building in St. Louis, Missouri, and raged out of control for more than twenty-
two hours. So intense was the inferno that people living nearby had to
remain indoors due to the heavy, acrid smoke that hung in the air. It was
only after the fire was extinguished four days later that the full extent of
the damage was known: eighteen million official military files were lost
in the blaze, including 80 percent of personnel discharge records from
1912 to 1960. No duplicate or microfilm copies of these records were ever
produced.

"Look, if they couldn't dig up anything on this guy, I doubt I'll have
any better luck."

"But you were in the 28th," Jeanly insisted. "There must be something
you can do back in America."

Frank's voice was lost with his thoughts as he looked one more time
at the pictures on the wall. *This will be impossible*, he thought. He stood
silent for a few moments, and then after a deep breath announced, "All
right, when I get back, I'll try to find him, but . . ."

"I know you'll do it," Jeanly interrupted as he patted Frank on the
shoulder. "I know you will find him."

Frank took a final look at each of the photographs, hoping that maybe
he had overlooked some detail that would reveal more about the tall, cos-
tumed man. But there was nothing. The three men turned to leave the
museum, and after only a few steps, Frank stopped abruptly. He glanced
back at the group of photos on the wall and then looked at Jeanly and
Raymond, his face awash with curiosity.

"Okay. But why?"

"Why?" Jeanly repeated, puzzled.

"Yes, why?" Frank asked again. "What's the deal with this guy?"

Raymond and Jeanly stared at each other, each waiting for the other
to answer. It wasn't that they didn't understand Frank's question, they
just hadn't expected it, and they didn't know what to say. For them, finding Richard Brookins seemed so natural. Jeanly shrugged.

"Why do we want to find him?" Raymond queried, still a bit startled.

"Well, yes. I mean, why are you so interested in finding him after all
this time?" Frank somehow felt that he had offended the two men, but he
wasn't sure exactly how.

"Ah," Raymond suddenly brightened, "because this is a special time in
Wiltz. We will soon celebrate the anniversary of our town—the rebuilding

of Wiltz after the war. It will be a very big celebration. That is why you must help us to find this man. We have a special project in mind."

Frank nodded. "A special project? I see." Although he didn't. "But I guess I'm wondering why you want to find *this* guy," Frank said pointing at the wall of photos. "What does he have to do with all of that?"

"Of course!" Jeanly finally understood, a proud smile stretching his face. "We need to find him because *he* is the American Saint Nicolas."

CHAPTER 4

1944

The 112th Infantry Regiment of the 28th Infantry Division was part of the Pennsylvania National Guard federalized into the US Army in 1942. Along with the 109th and 110th Regiments, they were known as the Keystone Division because of the red keystone-shaped shoulder patch insignia the men wore on their uniforms. In the months following the D-Day invasion, the division had fought its way through the French countryside and now, with Paris liberated and the Germans on the run, the Allies were racing toward Berlin.

The Keystone Division spent a much-needed night of relief billeted in Versailles, a few miles southwest of Paris along with the 4th Infantry Division ahead of their ceremonial role in helping the Parisians celebrate their liberation. Military command saw the occasion as an opportunity for publicity, and on August 29, 1944, they ordered the 28th, the only complete division in the vicinity, to march into Paris and join the festivities.

All along the streets, crowds gathered to cheer on the American and French soldiers as they made their way to the City of Lights. Once in Paris, the troops paraded before the frenzied masses that had gathered to celebrate after years of Nazi occupation. While exuberant cheers rang out, Army newsreel cameras rolled, capturing the historic moment and showing the people back home the fruits of the war effort. The cameras clicked away as row after row of the division's soldiers proudly marched through the Arc de Triomphe and down the Champs-Élysées.

In the days and weeks immediately following their march through Paris, the men of the Keystone Division were again called upon to fight the German army as it retreated out of France. September and October saw tough town-to-town fighting, as units of the 28th pushed their way through the Belgian countryside and on into Luxembourg. The Germans were being forced back to their well-defended homeland, a line that began in the Huertgen Forest.

The Huertgen Forest covers approximately fifty miles of the German-Belgian border south of the city of Aachen, Germany. One of the stated objectives of the American troops in the Huertgen was to take control of the dams on the Roer and Urft rivers. Allied command concluded that if the Germans controlled those dams, they could flood the forest valley below, delaying the Allied advance into Germany. The flooded lowlands would render any Allied tactical bridging useless and trap any US Army units that had forded the rivers. Troops cut off by the flooding could then be easily wiped out or captured by German reserves. The Allies also concluded that taking the Huertgen Forest would deny the German army a place to assemble a force large enough to counterattack the steadily advancing Allies. What the Allied commanders didn't know or didn't want to acknowledge was how well the Germans were already rooted in the Huertgen.

In peaceful times, the Huertgen Forest was a dark, ominous, almost medieval place. Its densely clustered fir and hardwoods towered overhead, and their thick lower branches entangled, making it nearly impossible to move through the hills without crouching close to the ground. To make matters worse, the trees always seemed to be dripping water, making the forest a challenge to firm footing on even the best days. The Germans took advantage of these natural obstacles and the ideal defensive terrain of deep gorges, high ridges, and narrow trails by digging into the heavily wooded hillside and creating a maze of well-concealed concrete bunkers and machine gun pillboxes protected by mine fields and concertina wire. It was in these deplorable conditions that the Allies chose to attack the entrenched Germans along the now-famous Siegfried line.

American troops began their initial attack in the mid-September, and by early October, whole divisions were committed to the battle. In the forest, the lattice of thick branches and the patches of fog, along with smoke from the exploding shells, made it difficult for the soldiers to see more than ten yards in any direction. Knee-deep mud—the result of more than a month of near-constant rain, sleet, and snow—rendered the few roads and logging trails snaking through the forest useless. As a

American soldiers advance into the Huertgen Forest, November 1944.
Photo: National Archives

result, providing armor and air support for the American soldiers was all but impossible. The soldiers also faced a near-constant cascade of German artillery shells pouring down on pre-sighted positions in the forest, while heavy machine gun and rifle fire from the bunkers and pillboxes raked the young and, in most cases, inexperienced troops as they tried to advance on the German positions through ribbons of barbed wire. The unremitting mortar and artillery fire decimated the ranks of the American troops, turning the otherwise peaceful forest into a valley of death. The waterlogged and heavily cratered forest floor was littered with downed trees and branches along with helmets, boots, canteens, broken rifles, machinery, torn and bloodied uniforms, and mangled bodies of dead and dying soldiers from both sides. Despite frontline reports that told of little or no progress in the attack at the expense of hundreds of lives per day, Allied commanders ordered that the advance continue.

Division after division was committed to the fight, and each time, the troops were torn to pieces. Replacement soldiers, some fresh off the boat from their training in England, were sent into the forest to reinforce battle-hardened but weary frontline troops. Most of the eager young soldiers were in their late teens or early twenties, and most of them never left the forest—some cut down within hours after arriving. Those that did survive had to cope not only with the slaughter that surrounded them but also with dysentery, near-epidemic trench foot, and (in some cases) even walking pneumonia brought on by wet clothes, cold food, little or no sleep, and no relief.

By mid-October after only a few weeks of fighting, the Americans lost nearly 80 percent of their frontline troops while making only minimal gains. Despite horrible battle conditions and mission creep, military command continued sending fresh soldiers to the front line to maintain the assault on the well-defended German positions.

In early November, battle conditions worsened with unrelenting rain giving way to sleet and snow. It was now the 28th Division's turn to join the fight. On November 2, units of the 28th launched an attack on Schmidt, a small town the Allies considered vital to securing a foothold in the Huertgen Forest. By nightfall of the next day, a battalion of the 112th Regiment had seized the town, but other battalions lagged behind in the fighting, and on November 4, German tanks and infantry counterattacked the fatigued, poorly supplied American troops, forcing them to retreat from Schmidt. In some of the bloodiest fighting the 28th Infantry Division would see during the entire war and under the most brutal of conditions, a battle waged nonstop for control of the town of Schmidt for the next three days.

Richard Brookins was a lanky, twenty-two-year-old corporal with the 28th Division. He was assigned as a cryptographer in the signal company's message center, and it was his unit's responsibility to keep the flow of communications, coded or otherwise, open throughout the war. Now, as German artillery pounded the American positions in the forested hills around Schmidt, all he could think about was keeping his arms close to his body and his back firmly pressed against the thick trunk of a pine tree. This time, the Germans were using proximity fuse shells. The shells would explode in the treetops, raining hot shards of metal and large heavy pieces of splintered wood down on the soldiers below. Many soldiers in the battle of the Huertgen Forest were killed not by bullets or hot shrapnel, but by the jagged falling timber that crushed or impaled. Rather than dive to the ground for cover as they had been trained to do, the GIs quickly learned that their best chance of surviving this type of artillery barrage was to plaster themselves against a tree. In doing so, the soldiers exposed only their thick steel helmets to the exploding treetops and shrapnel.

Brookins had been returning from an aid station after helping transport wounded soldiers. The men had tried to attack a German mortar position that was systematically firing on GIs who had dug into foxholes below the ridge. The German strategy was to expend one mortar round after another on an enemy position until they honed their coordinates, eventually killing all the soldiers huddled there. They would then direct their fire at the next position and repeat the process. Aside from the loss of life, the calculated attacks had a severe demoralizing effect on the American troops who were helpless to defend themselves.

Getting to the German mortar positions to stop the barrage was nearly impossible. To do so required crossing thirty yards of thickly mudded, densely wooded terrain: an area that had been pre-sighted by German mortar teams, allowing for easy and brutally accurate fire on the advancing troops. If the Americans managed to get past those first thirty yards, they faced an uphill attack against bunkers that had a clear field of cross fire from the moment the men left the cover of the woods. One of the wounded men was a lieutenant who had led an ill-fated assault. He had almost reached the bottom of the hill when another soldier set off a German S-mine. The S-mine was an anti-personnel mine that when triggered, launched a projectile into the air where it exploded, spraying the surrounding area with high-velocity steel balls. The young soldier was killed instantly—nearly torn in half, and the lieutenant was badly wounded. The rest of the men tried to continue the assault, but the well-fortified Germans quickly repelled them.

After helping at the aid station for most of the day, Brookins had made his way back to the captured pillbox that was now being used as a forward command post, all the while dodging enemy fire and skirting minefields. He was almost to the command post when the Germans began another artillery attack.

Shells began exploding in the treetops, this time only about thirty yards away. To Brookins, it seemed as though the barrage was aimed specifically at him. Three more bombs exploded in the treetops. He waited a few seconds for the fallout to clear and then ran to the pillbox that was now about sixty yards ahead of him. As he ran, the sights and sounds of battle engulfed him. Machine guns, rifle fire, mortar shells, artillery shells, exploding mines, yelling, screaming, and dying—all echoed through the darkening forest. As Brookins dashed across the last stretch to the bunker, the chaos ringing in his ears, he realized that he could have run right over a German position and never even known it was there. The Germans were everywhere, and Brookins couldn't see them or their positions through the dense forest and the thick smoke that hung in the air like a gray curtain.

He reached the pillbox and ducked inside, pausing for a few moments to catch his breath as the concussion of the nearby shells continued. He sat down wearily in a corner of the cement bunker—the same corner that had been his home for the past few days as he encoded and decoded messages amid the fighting that raged outside. At night, he would try to fight the trench foot the way many soldiers did, by removing his socks, flattening them, and placing them inside his shirt, where he hoped his body heat would dry them, or at least warm them by the next day. In the meantime, he'd remove the pair of socks that he had kept against his body that day and put them on before taking his sleeping bag outside the bunker. Once outside, Brookins would crawl into a dugout beneath some logs and try to rest for a few hours.

Another shell exploded, and then another, and then a third—each closer than the one before, with the last one hitting right outside the pillbox. The blast shook the earth around the bunker, sending debris and large, fragmented tree limbs to the ground. The pieces landed hard and then bounced off the roof of the bunker. Inside the pillbox, dust and dirt rained down from gaping cracks in the reinforced cement ceiling. Brookins instinctively huddled deeper into his corner, grabbing at the top of his helmet, trying to shield his radio and decoding equipment from the dust. When everything settled, Brookins quickly set about decoding the last message received. A few minutes later, the message the Keystone Division had been waiting for was in front of him. The 8th and 9th Infantry Divisions were gradually being deployed in relief of troops in the Huertgen Forest. Despite the good news, Brookins and the rest of the 28th Division would spend two more agonizing weeks in battle and incur more than six thousand casualties before relief came. So devastating were their losses that from then on, the German soldiers would refer to them as the "Bloody Bucket Division" in reference to their red keystone shoulder patches that the Germans said resembled buckets filled with blood.

Finally, in mid-November the Keystone Division was cycled out of the Huertgen battle and sent to the rear to regroup and rest. Brookins and the other members of the division's signal company message center were ordered to the division headquarters in a small Luxembourg town in the Ardennes called Wiltz.

CHAPTER 5

The town of Wiltz, along with the rest of Luxembourg, came under Nazi occupation in May of 1940. Luxembourg had remained neutral in the years preceding the war, with the government insisting that it was not a member of any alliance. The country only maintained a small volunteer army for ceremonial and educational functions, so when the Germans began their assault in Western Europe, it surprised no one that Luxembourg fell in less than a day. The Luxembourg government, along with Grand Duchess Charlotte, fled first to France and then by August 1940 to London, where a government-in-exile was formed. In Luxembourg the Germans declared martial law, and the *Wehrmacht* poured in, using Luxembourg as a stepping-stone for its advance through Belgium and on into France. Now in control of Western Europe, the German Army gave way to the Nazi party that took control of the small country's administration.

The Nazis considered Luxembourg to be part of the Third Reich and sought to erase all traces of its past while reeducating the population to believe they were ethnic Germans being welcomed back to the Fatherland. The name *Luxembourg* officially ceased to exist, and the country was instead called *Gau Moselland*, meaning "the country district." Social programs were introduced to "Germanize" the population. German laws were imposed. The speaking of *Lëtzebuergesch*, the native language, was outlawed. So, too, were all non-German holidays and customs. Street names, city names, and French surnames were converted to German names, and official licenses and documents were printed only in German.

Local protests against occupation and the new laws were short-lived. The Gestapo answered protests with harassment, beatings, imprisonment, and torture. Those who organized the protests, as well as some who participated, were sent to concentration camps as slave labor. Some were never seen again.

The Nazi oppression increased with the deportation of the country's small Jewish community, and then in 1942, the Germans began a program of forced conscription into the *Wehrmacht* for any Luxembourg male over the age of seventeen.

On August 31, 1942, people from all around Luxembourg who refused to adhere to Nazi policies and dictates banded together in a nationwide strike. The strike began in Wiltz, with the entire workforce at the town's leather factory walking off the job. Word of the strike spread quickly, spurred by the actions of town officials Michel Worré and Nicolas Müller who refused to work at their administrative positions at the town hall. Waves of resistance rolled through Luxembourg, reaching the central post office in Luxembourg City by early afternoon and eventually disrupting the distribution of mail that evening and the following day. Throughout the country, schoolchildren were kept out of school, teachers refused to teach, shop owners refused to open their doors, and laborers refused to work. In short, the country came to a standstill. Infuriated, the Nazis responded quickly by rounding up as many of the organizers and sympathizers as they could find. In Wiltz, four of the strike leaders arrested were respected teachers. They, along with others, were put on trial by a hastily assembled tribunal and sentenced to death. In a public display, the condemned were marched through town to waiting transport trucks and taken to the Hinzert concentration camp.

On September 2, 1942, at 6:30 p.m. Michel Worré and Nicolas Müller were marched in front of a wall at Hinzert. "Long live Luxembourg!" they yelled before a volley of bullets tore into them. The following day, the four teachers Charles Meyers, Josy Ewen, Alfred Brück, and Célestin Lommel were also executed. Their bodies and all the others executed because of the strike were buried in an unmarked grave. Their families, including their children, were subsequently rounded up and send to slave labor camps. The Luxembourg general strike that began in Wiltz was over.

In the end, such brutal treatment only succeeded in strengthening the opposition to German rule. A network of Luxembourg resistance groups was formed, operating throughout the country to aid downed

Allied flyers, hide soon-to-be conscripted youths, or organize clandestine operations to harass and disrupt the German war machine. In early September 1944, after several more skirmishes with the advancing Allies, the retreating *Wehrmacht* finally fled Luxembourg. After nearly four years of Nazi occupation, the people of Luxembourg—their spirits once again soaring—joyfully welcomed their American liberators. Soon, thousands of soldiers rotating through the country on R & R came to know Luxembourg as a paradise for war-weary troops.

What was left of the 28th Infantry Division limped into Wiltz a few days before Thanksgiving. Prior to the war, Wiltz's rich history and tranquil surroundings had made it a favorite destination for European vacationers. Now it was the perfect spot for the battered 28th Division not just because the division was headquartered there but also as a reserve area located far enough from the frontline fighting to allow the men to forget about the war—if only for a short time.

The men of the Keystone Division took advantage of the serene surroundings to collect themselves. Their daily duties included digging foxholes or manning forward lookout posts on the outskirts of town or off-loading supply trucks. But it was all easy duty compared to the fierce fighting still raging in the Huertgen Forest. When they finished their assignments, the men would enjoy hot meals and showers, clean clothes, passes to Paris, movies, and letters from home.

Headquarters for the 28th Division was in a large private home known as Villa Adler (named after its owner—the manager of the leather factory and a Jew, forced to flee Luxembourg prior to the German occupation). It had a sweeping westward view and stood majestically amongst the other buildings surrounding it. Villa Adler was a short walk down the street from the Hotel Bellevue. Featuring a grand entranceway with marble floors, ornate fireplaces, and large rooms it had also served as German headquarters before liberation.

Most of the time, Corporal Brookins' daily duty found him in the basement of Villa Adler in front of a SIGABA cryptography machine in the communication center, working on encoding or decoding messages. During downtime, as was the case with most of soldiers, he would catch up on letter writing, play cards, smoke, and dream of home. Brookins was also one of only two men in all of Luxembourg responsible for showing movies to the soldiers on R & R. Back in basic training, Brookins had been given the assignment of caring for two RCA 16-mm film projectors—two in case one was lost or Brookins needed to swap out parts in order to keep at least one functional. He used them to show training films as well as the latest Hollywood movies, when available. For months after landing on the beaches of Normandy, he hadn't even seen a projector; now at Division HQ, he was once again the man behind the movies, and he awaited orders to travel to various towns with his screen and projector in tow.

On Thanksgiving Day, Brookins had set up the projector in the dining hall of the Hotel Bellevue. The room had been converted into a makeshift mess hall, with the field kitchen opposite the hotel on the Rue de la Fontaine. After the men feasted on their holiday meal, Brookins planned to once again show the movie *Going My Way*—a film he'd carried since leaving England, where he hadn't the time to swap movies at the film exchange in London prior to debarkation to the continent.

He sat near his equipment at the end of a long table in the crowded mess hall, his mess kit filled with makeshift Thanksgiving fare. The mood in the dining room was light. The men laughed and joked, all the while knowing how much they had to be thankful for on this particular Thanksgiving holiday.

"Brooks! Hey, Brooks!" a voice called from the end of the food line.

Brookins looked up to see Cpl. Harry Stutz calling to him. Stutz was also in the division's signal company and worked alongside Brookins at the message center along with two other soldiers: Frank Duffy of Cincinnati, Ohio, and Ray Hammerstedt of Jamestown, New York. They shared an assigned room in a house on the Grande Rue. Solidly built, of average height with thick, black hair and soft but narrow eyes, Stutz's face looked fuller than it actually was thanks to an apparently perpetual smile that arched the flesh in his cheeks. It was the sort of smile that always made him appear mischievous; as if he had a secret or knew the answer before everyone else—as if his thoughts were always elsewhere, restless, planning. In reality, it was the smile of a tireless optimist, always trying to find the good side of every person or situation, even though that was becoming more difficult as the war dragged on.

Brookins raised a forkful of reconstituted powdered potatoes in a gesture of acknowledgement. Stutz began weaving his way through the men, back-slapping and trading one-liners with the others on his way past the tables.

"What are you up to, Brooks? Mind if I sit?" Stutz kidded, and without waiting for an answer, he placed his mess kit down on the table and swung his leg over the bench. "Great stuff, huh?" Stutz said acerbically about the food. "You'd think that this being a holiday, we'd have had some decent chow around here. I'm starting to think that maybe the cooks are really working for the Krauts. I swear I'm getting ready to shoot them myself." He paused to shove a hunk of gravy-laden spam, a sorry substitute for turkey, into his mouth. "So, what's the movie tonight?"

"*Going My Way*. It's a Bing Crosby movie. You gonna stick around to watch it?"

"Sure, why not? It's not like my dance card is filled," Stutz joked while mixing together everything on his tin. Brookins laughed through his latest mouthful and then smiled and nodded toward the projector.

"I think you'll like it. I've already seen it a bunch of times. It's a good movie for the holidays."

"Yeah, some holiday being here," Stutz said solemnly, the perpetual smile fading.

A conspicuous silence fell between the two men amidst the din of the mess hall. Brookins knew what Stutz meant without having to ask; surely they would rather be home with their families, not just for Thanksgiving but also for the upcoming Christmas holiday, or in Stutz's case, Hanukkah. More important, they realized that they were there enjoying a holiday meal while so many others, so many brave, honor-bound and frightened friends were still fighting in the Huertgen Forest. And there were the others—those friends who never came out of the Huertgen.

Suddenly, as if startled awake from a nap, Stutz shook his head and looked up at Brookins, the smile once again carving into his face.

"Speaking of holidays, I see Christmas is just around the corner."

"Christmas?" Brookins chortled, wondering why Stutz would be asking about the Christian holiday. "I thought Hanukkah started first, no? Isn't that right around the corner?" he continued, opening the door to the conversation he knew Harry wanted to have.

"Sure, sure. In a couple of weeks. Plenty of time for you to pick me up something nice. You've got my sizes, right?" Harry joked. Brookins laughed a "Yeah, right" and dug for another forkful.

"I look at it this way: it all happens around the same time, right?" Stutz charged ahead, the tone of genuine excitement evident. "But let me tell you this. I'll bet you didn't know that the people here in Wiltz haven't had much of a Christmas, or anything else for that matter, since the Krauts took over. Did you know that?"

"No, I guess I never really thought about it," Brookins answered, his eyebrows raised with genuine surprise, his thoughts a swirl. He began to think about the war, how long it had lasted, and how long the Germans had occupied Luxembourg and the rest of Europe. But then his mind quickly wandered to how long he'd been in the war, and he began to think about last year's Christmas, when he was stationed in England. Brookins had celebrated Christmas with the rest of the men from the 28th Division's Signal Company Message Center. The men did what they could to make it feel like a real Christmas: they got a tree and decorated it, sang Christmas carols, had a traditional Christmas dinner, and opened gifts and mail sent by their families back in the States. When all that was done, the men had begun drinking, not just to celebrate but also as a way of trying to forget where they were—or more exactly, where they were not: at home.

"Well, I was thinking that since they haven't had much to celebrate in the way of Christmas or anything else, and since it looks like we're gonna be stuck here, maybe we could have some sort of party. A Christmas party. What do you think?" Stutz's question jarred Brookins from his thoughts.

Brookins raised his eyebrows again and leaned back on the bench as if a strong wind had just blown against him. He sat looking at Stutz in disbelief.

"Did I hear you right? A Christmas party?"

"Sure! Why not?"

"Why not? Wait, let me get this straight," said Brookins, his delivery clipped. "*You*—a good little Jewish boy from the Midwest—want to have a Christmas party here in Luxembourg in a town full of Catholics. Am I missing something?"

"What's the matter? Don't you like Christmas?" Harry countered.

"Sure, I like Christmas, but that's not the point. And in case you haven't noticed, there's this little thing call a war going on."

"Exactly," Stutz said. "That's it right there. That's the whole reason we should have a party in the first place! Because of this whole filthy mess. Look, it's the holiday season, and we're stuck here. Why not have a party or something? Besides *this town* could use it."

"This town? What do you mean 'this town'?"

"Well sure, the party would be for the town too. In fact it'd be mostly for the town, but for us too," explained Stutz.

"Harry, hang on," Brookins pleaded. "First of all, we're not even supposed to talk to these people, remember? Don't *fraternize*. That's the word. And now you want to throw a Christmas party?"

"Don't fraternize," Stutz mocked. "Are you kidding me? These people aren't working for the Krauts. C'mon, Brooks, look around. They hate the Germans more than we do!"

"Is that so? How do you figure?" Brookins asked, his disbelief genuine.

"Well, I figure from talking to this guy I met in town. His name is Schneider. Martin Schneider. We got to talking one day, and he invited me over to his house for dinner. Now I go over almost every night. And get this: not only does he cure his own ham and make his own sausage, but this guy also makes homemade schnapps or brandy or moonshine or whatever you want to call it. He makes it from apples. It's great stuff, Brooks. It'll take the chill out of you, that's for sure. Probably strip the paint off a tank too for that matter. You should come over and try it one of these nights."

"Harry?" Brookins said, steering the conversation back on course.

"What?"

His dinner finished, Brookins slid his mess kit to the side and pulled out a cigarette pack from his left breast pocket. He fished one out, tucked it into the corner of his mouth then patted his pockets in search of his Zippo. Harry got to his first and offered a light.

"You were saying?" Brookins said through an exhale of smoke.

"Oh, about them hating the Krauts? Well, as it turns out, this guy Schneider was a member of the resistance here in Luxembourg. From what he tells me, life in Wiltz with the Germans was no picnic. They had it pretty bad. In fact, he and some of the other members of the resistance arranged some sort of a strike or protest against the Nazis. I don't know the whole story, but I guess it was a countrywide thing. Everyone was in on it, and it started right here in Wiltz." Harry paused long enough to load another forkful of food and shove it into his mouth. "Anyway," Stutz continued, his tone more somber, "the Krauts came down hard on the town. They gathered up the people they thought organized the thing and maybe even some who didn't, threw them onto some trucks, and drove out of town. They were never seen again. From what I gather, they were interrogated and shot. The Krauts just dumped their bodies in some pit. Hey, remember those posters we saw? The ones with the black print and red background?" Stutz quizzed and Brookins nodded. "Well, the Krauts printed them so everyone would know what had happened. These guys had been rounded up and shot. They plastered them all over the place."

The poster displayed after the general strike that began in Wiltz. It reads, "The state court has sentenced to death because of the insurrection hazard to German military construction work in Luxembourg by strike the following people . . ."

Brookins lowered his head, shaking it from side to side. It was another account of Nazi brutality from another liberated European town. Each time Brookins heard a story, it affected him; it made him wonder how the Germans could treat innocent people so cruelly.

"Well, this guy Schneider managed to escape and go into hiding," Harry continued. "He only came back when we liberated the country. So believe me, these people ain't spying for the Germans. They hate 'em."

"No kidding?" Brookins said, soaking it all in with genuine interest. "So I guess you've been over to this guy's house quite a bit."

"Yeah, like I said, just about every night. I worked it out with the cooks so I can bring him and his wife all of our leftovers and garbage."

"Our garbage?" Brookins asked hesitantly.

"Sure. No, it's not for them. The garbage is for the pigs!" Stutz stammered. "He feeds the pigs the stuff we throw out. Like I said, you should taste his ham!"

"*Ham* and *sausage*? Harry?" Brookins needled.

"Well, like you said, there's a war going on. One has to sacrifice. Don't worry, I'll square it with my rabbi when I get home," Stutz said with an eye roll.

"Look, Harry. I get it. It's been tough times here. It's been tough all over the place. But what does any this have to do with you wanting to throw a Christmas party?"

"Keep your shirt on. I'm getting to that. Well, we got to talking one night, and that's when I met his niece, Martha. Brooks, you should have seen her. She's the cutest thing. She couldn't have been more than seven or eight years old. She'd have melted your heart. Anyway, this guy Martin told me that here in Wiltz, the people—well, the kids really—haven't had much of a Christmas to celebrate in the past four or five years thanks to the Krauts. And actually, what's an even bigger holiday around here is Saint Nicolas Day."

"What's Saint Nicolas Day?" Brookins quizzed.

"Yeah, I guess it's pretty big here. This Saint Nicolas is their version of Santa Claus. From what I gather, Christmas here is a family event. People do their own thing, but Saint Nicolas Day is a whole other story. It's town-wide celebration, and it actually takes place a couple of weeks or so before Christmas. Anyway, the kids here in town haven't seen Saint Nicolas or Christmas or whatever in almost *five* years. There're probably some kids who were so young when the Nazis took over that they don't even know who Saint Nicolas is. And that's just it. It's the kids I really feel sorry for," Stutz said, stabbing at his mashed potatoes with his fork. "No Christmas or anything for almost five years? Can you imagine? It's nuts."

Brookins shrugged and shook his head, "No, I can't." He took a long drag from his nearly finished cigarette, and as he breathed out, he stared at the blue smoke, thinking about what Harry had just said. An entire town, even an entire country, prohibited from celebrating their holidays, especially Christmas. It made no sense. But then this was war, Brookins thought, and in war a lot of things just didn't make sense.

"So this guy Schneider said it's looking like there won't be much for them to celebrate this year either," Stutz continued. "I mean, sure they can celebrate Saint Nicolas Day and Christmas, but they don't have anything, you know, because of the war. There's nothing to give the kids. *Nothing*," he stressed, looking away as his emotions got the better of him. He quickly collected himself, and with his familiar broad smile looked back at Brookins.

"So I was thinking that maybe *we* could throw a little party—a Christmas party—for us and them, but mostly for them. The kids. For them, it'd be a Saint Nicolas party."

"It sounds good and all, Harry, but I don't think the brass are gonna go along with it," Brookins said, sensing how much the idea meant to Stutz.

Stutz looked at Brookins and smiled even wider. "They already have. The Old Man already signed off on it."

"What? Hang on a sec," Brookins launched in astonishment. "You're telling me that with everything that's going on, General Cota okayed throwing a party—a Christmas party—here in Wiltz?"

"Not only did he okay it, but he also thought it was a great idea. Said it was just the thing this town and the whole division needs," Stutz beamed.

"Wait, you spoke to Cota?" Brookins questioned in disbelief.

"Well, not in person," Harry admitted somewhat sheepishly. "I got the idea and talked to Sergeant Teterus about it. He said it was fine by him but I should run it by First Sergeant Fernandez. So that's just what I did, and he said he was okay with it and that he'd bring it up to the captain. Well it must have kept going up from there because Teterus told me this morning that we got the go-ahead."

"I don't believe it!" Brookins gaped.

"Believe it, buddy. Cota's even going to write a greeting or something on the invitations."

"Invitations? What invitations? You're going to pass out invitations to this thing? Who are you going to hand them to and how?"

"Sure, why not? Nothing too fancy, but it has to be in English and of course their language, whatever it's called. It's not German or French. Something in between I guess. Luxembourg-ese. Anyway, Martin said he could translate for us. His English is pretty good. And if he can't, we can get the teachers to do it. As for getting them out, well, we'll just go door-to-door if that's what it takes. I mean, ain't like the town's that big."

"Unbelievable . . . ," Brookins cut in. "There's a war going on all around, and you—*you* want to have a Christmas party. Now that's rich. Let me ask, does your rabbi know what you're up to?" Brookins kidded again. The more Harry spoke, spilling details, the more dumbfounded Brookins became. "So I'm guessing you've put a lot of thought into this whole thing."

"No, not really. It just sort of came to me the other day. But getting back to those invitations, Brooks, can we do that? I mean, do we have the stuff to print up some sort of invitation? And if we do, any idea on how long it would take? The reason I ask is because this Saint Nicolas Day, well it's only about ten days from now. December sixth."

Brookins thought for a minute about the equipment the message center had at its disposal. "I don't know. I'm pretty sure we don't have that kind of stuff here, but maybe I'm wrong. Hamann's the guy to ask."

"Well, if we don't have the capability, that's all right. Martin said he could get the printer in town to do it."

Brookins sat back, shaking his head. He snickered while sizing up his friend.

"I still can't believe you got the old man 'Dutch' Cota himself to give this his stamp of approval. That's pretty good. We go from 'no fraternizing' straight to throwing them a party! Only you, Harry. Only you."

"Typical, right?" Stutz laughed.

"Situation normal . . ." Brookins started.

"Yeah, I know the rest," Stutz finished.

The two shared a laugh as Stutz glanced over at the projector.

"Hey, what did you say the name of the picture is?"

CHAPTER 6

In Luxembourg, the legend of the *Kleeschen*, or Saint Nicolas, is a centuries-old tradition. It tells of an evil butcher who killed three children, intending to turn them into sausage. But with the help of God, Saint Nicolas brought the children back to life and killed the evil butcher. According to tradition, on the night of December 5, Saint Nicolas and his helper *Houseker*, or Black Peter, enter all the houses in town to bring the children presents. In the days preceding his visit, the children put their shoes, originally made of wood, on windowsills or by their bedroom doors. When the *Kleeschen* makes his rounds on the eve of Saint Nicolas Day, he leaves chocolates, candy, or other sweets in the shoes of children who deserve presents. Meanwhile, *Houseker,* dressed head to toe in coarse black garments, carries sticks to punish those children who have misbehaved throughout the year.

After talking with Martin Schneider and his little niece Martha about Christmas and Saint Nicolas Day, Harry Stutz calculated that it had been almost five years since any celebration had taken place in the town, and he was determined not to let another holiday pass unobserved.

Gen. Norman "Dutch" Cota, the commander of the 28th Infantry Division, thought that throwing a Christmas party for the people of Wiltz would not only raise the spirits of the townspeople, but following the devastating losses in the Huertgen, it would also help lift the morale of the men in the division. It might even make for a good PR opportunity, so the official Army newspaper, the *Stars and Stripes,* sent someone to Wiltz to do a story about the party.

After getting the go-ahead from command, Corporal Stutz gathered a small group of men from the Message Center and formed a makeshift committee to handle the party plans. Saint Nicolas Day was less than a week away, and there were many things that needed to be done if the party was going to take place. Stutz assigned one of the men the task of getting the invitations written and translated and then printed by Jempy Meyers and Fränzen Schneider, the printers in Wiltz. Once printed, the invitations would be delivered to the teachers at the schools who would then see to it that each child took one home. Two of the committee soldiers were put in charge of collecting as much chocolate and candy as they could from the other Message Center soldiers. The plan was to start with the men assigned to the message center and then branch out to other soldiers in the signal company. Stutz assigned the remaining committee members the task of getting together with the company cooks and informing them of the party plans with enough lead time to bake cakes and make doughnuts for the party. The baked treats then needed to be taken from the field kitchen to the party, wherever that would be. The soldiers would also see to it that collected D-bars, the bitter chocolate bars made specifically for GI rations, would be delivered to the nuns at the castle, where they would be melted and used to make hot chocolate for the children. Stutz took upon himself the task of finding a time and place for the party. He thought of two possible sources of assistance: the priest at the local church and the principal of the school. Stutz reasoned that in this predominately Catholic country, the head of the local church (in this case Father Wolff) could prove invaluable. Stutz also thought that since the party was intended mainly for the children, the school principal or some of the teachers might be able to help coordinate the activities.

Stutz hiked up the street from HQ and through Wiltz to the church near the center of town. Inside, he spotted Father Wolff, a bearded, middle-aged man dressed in a black robe, sweeping the floors of the church with a broom so old that its tattered bristles were worn away to a forty-five degree angle.

The priest turned as he heard the heavy wooden door close behind him. Stutz waved a hello and began walking toward the priest. Then, suddenly embarrassed, he quickly removed the helmet he'd worn into the building.

"*Gudde Moien*," said Stutz—which was the only Lëtzebuergesch he'd picked up since he arrived in Wiltz—followed with "Hello, Father."

He spoke slowly, clearly, and a bit nervously, not knowing if the priest spoke English. If he didn't, Stutz wasn't sure how he was going to communicate his idea for the party. He was also a bit nervous because, although he'd seen more than his share of churches as the 28th made their way through Europe, as a Jew he had little cause to be in one other than to clear it of the enemy or as a place to grab some sleep. Besides, most of the churches the soldiers came across were either heavily battle damaged or bombed to rubble, yet here in Wiltz, even the stained glass windows remained intact. Stutz was relieved to hear Father Wolff greet him in English, albeit with a thick accent. Without thinking, Stutz extended his hand to Father Wolff, but as he did so, his mind raced, wondering if it was proper to shake hands with a priest. He wondered if he had unintentionally insulted the priest or broken some religious taboo. Stutz was again noticeably relieved when Father Wolff took his hand. The two men exchanged introductions, and Stutz asked the priest if he had a few minutes to talk. Father Wolff smiled and nodded as he motioned to Stutz to sit down in one of the pews.

"What is it that I can do for you?" Father Wolff asked through his thick accent.

"Well, I'm not exactly sure how to put this," Stutz began, but then he saw the puzzled expression on Father Wolff's face and realized that he might be speaking too quickly. He paused for a second, feigned a cough as if clearing his throat and then continued, this time his speech more measured.

"Father, I was hoping that you could help me with an idea I had for a Christmas party—for the town."

"Pardon me?" Father Wolff asked, his face clouding over with bewilderment.

"Well, yes. A Christmas party, I guess you'd call it, when everyone gets together to celebrate the season. Christmas, or whatever," Harry shrugged matter-of-factly, explaining the concept.

"Yes, of course," Father Wolff smiled. "I understand, but what I am wondering is why? Why do you want to do this?"

"Oh," Stutz said, realizing that he'd misread the priest's expression. "Well, I was speaking to Martin Schneider. Do you know him?" Stutz asked but continued without waiting for a reply. "Well, he told me about Christmas and the whole Saint Nicolas thing here in Wiltz and about the Germans," Stutz said, knowing that the priest would understand the reference to the Nazi occupation. "So I was thinking that maybe we could help bring back or at least help celebrate Saint Nicolas Day."

Father Wolff sat back in the pew as he thought for a few moments about what Corporal Stutz had just said. Once he was sure he had understood Stutz, his face began to light up with excitement at the idea. Stutz saw the priest's obvious delight and proceeded to explain the party preparations that had already been set into motion. Then, with Stutz encouraging his input, Father Wolff suggested that the party be held at the castle at the other end of town. At the castle, tables could be set up for the food provided by the company cooks. Stutz nodded in agreement at the priest's suggestions.

Father Wolff then volunteered more details surrounding the traditions of Saint Nicolas Day. Stutz was surprised to learn that besides the legend of Saint Nicolas, there was also an actual Saint Nicolas who had lived in the second century. *That* Saint Nicolas, through his deeds of helping children, became the patron saint not only of children but also of sailors and robbers. Stutz was a bit confused by the reference to robbers, but Father Wolff explained as best he could with his limited English that in the days of land barons and feudal lords, a robber was a person who stole from the wealthy to provide for those in need.

Listening to Father Wolff explain how the Saint Nicolas Day celebrations had evolved throughout the years, Stutz realized more than ever that his Christmas party was becoming a celebration of *their* Saint Nicolas Day. It was also shaping up to be the largest event the tiny town had celebrated since their liberation three months earlier.

Stutz stood up from the pew and this time shook the priest's hand without hesitation, thanking him for his help and suggestions. He walked to the front of the church, his step buoyed with excitement. Stutz placed his helmet on his head, leaned into one of the heavy wooden doors, and stepped into the winter air. The door had almost closed behind him when he turned his head, gave a final nod to the priest and bounded down the stairs.

All that was left now was to settle on a time for the celebration. Stutz trekked down the hill again, past Villa Adler to the public school where he met with the principal and several other English-speaking teachers. Stutz introduced himself and explained his party plans to the teachers, who were overjoyed at the proposal. After a brief discussion amongst each other in Lëtzebuergesch, the teachers suggested to Stutz that the festivities begin at six o'clock in the afternoon to accommodate the school schedules, both there and at the girl's school at the convent. They also suggested that after briefly meeting the children at the public school, the actual party could take place inside the castle, where there were rooms large enough to accommodate all the children, parents, and teachers. Finally, the teachers convinced Harry that the party should be held on the eve of Saint Nicolas Day—December fifth—rather than on the sixth, saying that it would be more in line with holiday tradition. Armed with the background knowledge provided by Father Wolff, Stutz agreed with the time, date, and place of the party and told the teachers that invitations would be forthcoming. The teacher's faces registered a look of surprise when Stutz mentioned the invitations. They again talked amongst themselves, and Stutz soon realized that they were making sure they had understood him correctly. Moments later, the teacher whose English was best of the three spoke up. She began slowly, wanting to get the translation right.

"You said *invitations*, yes? There are to be invitations?"

"Yes, that's right. We'll get them to you as soon as we get them printed. I was hoping you could then give them to the children," Stutz said. Again the teachers talked in hushed voices amongst themselves, occasionally glancing at Harry, who was standing nervously silent.

"Yes. We will make sure the children get them," she spoke again, a slight quiver to her voice. "Thank you for all you are doing." The teachers all smiled and nodded appreciatively.

As he left the school, Stutz was suddenly overcome by a feeling of uneasiness. The enormity of what this Christmas party—this Saint Nicolas party—was going to mean to the town finally hit him. He turned to look back at the school and at the teachers who were still standing at the front door and realized why the teachers had been so surprised at the mention of invitations. The people of Wiltz had been prohibited from celebrating Saint Nicolas Day for more than four years, and now, here he was telling them that not only would there be a Saint Nicolas Day celebration, but there would be formal invitations as well.

Harry dug his fists deep into his jacket pockets and braced himself against the frigid breeze sweeping through Wiltz. As he walked, he couldn't help thinking about the party and its meaning. A sudden cold gust wrapped around him, but he never felt it. All Harry could feel was the knot in the pit of his stomach. He thought of the children of Wiltz; how their faces, like the face of eight-year-old Martha Schneider, would light up when they were given the candies and chocolates and whatever else could be scrounged up such on short notice. Stutz smiled to himself as the knot in his stomach disappeared.

He'd walked only a short distance before he found himself standing at the steps leading from the street to the front door at HQ. Harry was satisfied that the party plans were beginning to fall into place. However, based on his conversations with Father Wolff and the teachers, there was one more detail to address and one more stop he needed to make. It was something that he hadn't given any prior thought to, simply because he didn't know the details of the Saint Nicolas tradition. Now he realized that it was the biggest detail of them all.

He took a deep breath of cold air and then sprinted up the stairs towards the two MPs standing guard at the entrance. Stutz had gone up only a few steps when one of the double doors opened and Corporal Brookins stepped outside.

"Brooks," Stutz called excitedly, "you're just the guy I'm looking for!"

"Oh, yeah? Why's that?" Brookins was only half listening as he bundled against the cold.

"I just came from the school," Harry thumbed over his shoulder. "I was talking with some of the teachers there about the Saint Nicolas Party."

"The what?" asked Brookins. "Oh, you mean the Christmas party thing you were talking about? How's that going?"

"So far, so good. Actually that's what I wanted to talk to you about. Have you got a minute? What do you say we get some coffee?" Stutz suggested tugging at Brookins' coat sleeve, urging him down the stairs.

"Sure, why not? I could use a cup of joe."

As the two men walked up the street to the Bellevue Hotel and the mess hall, Stutz searched for a way to ease into the conversation.

"Cold today, but not as bad as I thought it would be," he said.

"No. It's actually kind of nice. It sort of reminds me of the winters back home in Rochester. If it's not snowing and the sun's out, that is. The problem is, it's usually snowing."

The two men stepped inside the mess hall, Stutz chuckling at Brookins' reminiscing and then with obvious purpose, changing the subject.

"Listen, Brooks, about this party. Did I mention that I've got guys working on all the arrangements?"

Brookins nodded, but it didn't matter because Stutz wasn't looking at him and didn't wait for a response.

"Well, we formed this sort of makeshift committee, and the guys are working on different things. Sergeant Teterus is going to be handling the invitations with the printer in town, which reminds me that I need to get the details to him ASAP, and Hamann's talking to the cooks about getting stuff made—cakes, cookies, or whatever they can whip up—that sort of thing, and Burton and Duffy are going around collecting chocolate and candy from any of the guys who want to contribute," Stutz babbled as he ladled near-boiling coffee from the large pot at the end of the chow line into a metal mess kit cup.

As Brookins began filling a cup for himself, Stutz took a sip of his black coffee, nearly burning his lips. He tried to cool the liquid by blowing on it and between breaths said to Brookins in a tone of utter humility, "I was hoping you'd give us a hand too."

"I was kind of wondering if you were going to get around to me. Seemed like you have everyone else involved *but* me," said Brookins feigning insult. He wrapped his hands around the cup to keep them warm and copied Stutz by blowing across the surface of the piping-hot liquid. Although he preferred cream and sugar in his coffee, he'd gotten used to drinking it black because both those items were usually nowhere to be found. "Sure, Harry. I'll give you a hand. No problem," Brookins said settling into a chair at one of the long tables. "I've got a bunch of candy sitting with my gear. I really don't eat it except for the gum, but it's all yours. Take it," Brookins said matter-of-factly, though he wondered why Stutz, who had seated himself across from Brookins, seemed so uneasy about asking for something, especially since he'd offered to help with the party a few days earlier. "All right, take the gum too, but I'll keep my smokes, if you don't mind," he grinned.

The two men laughed, and then Brookins added, "I'll get the all the stuff for you a little later."

"Thanks, Brooks, that's great. And believe me, we'll take it all off your hands. Except for the smokes, that is. But that's not what I had in mind. I was thinking you could help us out in another way," Stutz said looking Brookins directly in the eye.

"What other way?" Brookins asked skeptically, thinking that if Stutz was being this direct, whatever he wanted was going to be big.

Stutz took off his helmet and scratched nervously at the top of his head while looking down toward the floor. He took a deep breath, smoothed down his hair, and looked back up at Brookins.

"We need someone to be Saint Nicolas," he finally blurted out and then watched as a look of shock seeped over Brookins' face.

Brookins squinted and leaned in closer to Stutz, as if he hadn't fully understood.

"Wait, what? Are you serious?" he said, eyebrows arched. "Hold on. You mean me?" he asked in a soft voice, not knowing what else to say but thinking he had to say something. He knew full well that Stutz was serious.

"Look, Brooks, remember that whole Saint Nicolas tradition I told you about? Well, it turns out we need someone to play Saint Nicolas for the kids. Come on. It'll be easy. Just like playing Santa Claus."

"Sure, it'll be easy, but I'm not the guy. Look, I've never played Santa Claus, or Kris Kringle or St. Nick or anyone else for that matter."

"Come on. It'll be a snap. All you have to do is meet the kids, shake their hands, give 'em a pinch on the cheek, a pat on the head, and send them on their way. It'll be easy."

"A snap?" Brookins protested. "If it's going to be such a snap, why don't you do it?"

"Because I'm coordinating everything, making sure everything's in place and on schedule. What do you want me to do? Stop everything to be St. Nick?"

"Okay. Well, then why not one of the other guys? Look, you told me at dinner the other night that this is a big thing to these people, right? No Christmas, no Saint Nicolas Day or whatever, all because of the Krauts, right? Didn't you say that?" Brookins was pleading now. "Well, what if I screw this up? This being such a big deal around here, what if I screw it up somehow? What if I forget to smile at some kid or something? These people will never forget it!"

"Brooks, there's nothing to screw up," Stutz emphasized calmingly. "All you have to do is just meet the kids, let them see you in the costume and . . ."

"Costume?" Brookins' voice hit a noticeably higher pitch. "What costume? You never mentioned anything about a costume. What costume?" His brow furrowed.

"Seriously, Brooks, what did you think? Saint Nicolas would be walking around town in army issues and a steel helmet? Of course there's a costume involved, which is why I need you," Stutz said reaching across the table and putting his hand on Brookins' shoulder to calm him. "Look,

I spoke to the local priest. His name's Father Wolff. He's going to let us use his mass robes for you to wear, and he's about your height. You're the only guy who can fit in them."

"Right, Harry. The only guy?" Brookins knew perfectly well that there were plenty of other guys his height.

"All right, all right. Sure there're other guys who could fit the robes, no question. But Brooks, would I trust them to pull this off? You're right, I did say this is a big deal to these people and it is. I'm not going to lie to you. After talking to the priest and some of the teachers at the school, I realized that it's shaping up to be a very big deal, especially for these kids, which is why I don't trust just anyone to do this. Come on, what do you say? It's for the kids."

Now Harry was pleading. Brookins stared at Stutz for a few moments, not knowing what he should say or do. He blinked his gaze away from Harry, sat back in his chair, and looked about the mess hall, focusing on nothing. When Brookins first heard about the party idea, he thought Harry was going through the motions just to get out of doing any real duty because he'd be spending his time running around organizing the party and milking it for all the free time he could. He even had the blessing of command. It would be the perfect gold-bricking scheme. Now, however, Brookins saw the passion in Harry's eyes and heard the sincerity in his tone. It was obvious that no matter the reason he'd started down this road, Harry Stutz had put his true heart into this party for the GIs, yes, but really for the children.

Brookins' thoughts quickly shifted to Christmas and about not being home again with his family or with Virginia, his fiancée. He thought about the friends he'd made since joining the army and of those he'd lost since they arrived in Europe; he thought about the Huertgen. He thought about things that happened here in Wiltz during the Nazi occupation and about the children of Wiltz, and he thought about the little bit of joy they might get from this Saint Nicolas Day and from seeing Saint Nicolas in the flesh.

Brookins removed his helmet, placing it on the table with a thud. He wrapped a hand around the back of his neck and squeezed, and then he looked back at Harry patiently sipping at his coffee, waiting. Brookins pressed his lips into tight smile, took in a deep breath, and at the end of a long sigh, he nodded and heard himself say, "Okay. What do I have to do?"

CHAPTER 7

Preparations for the Christmas party were well underway, and now that Harry knew the time and the place, he could concentrate on the invitations. He jotted down a few phrases on a scrap of paper, changing and rephrasing them several times until he had the wording just right. He then visited the home of Martin Schneider, where, over several glasses of homemade schnapps, he had Martin translate the words into Lëtzebuergesch. On the morning of December 1, Stutz tracked down Sgt. Frank Teterus and handed the paper to him with instructions to have the invitations printed in both languages. The actual design of the invitation he left to the printer in town. A few hours later, the invitations were ready, and the assigned men distributed them to the schools for distribution. The invitations read

THE 28TH SIGNAL CO
MESSAGE CENTER SECTION
is happy to have the children of Wiltz,
Luxembourg, as their guests for our
Santa Claus Party
On Tuesday, December 5, 1944,
in the large room of the
PENSIONNAT
from 6–8 p.m.

December 5, 1944, was a cold, damp, and windy day in Wiltz, but still a sense of anticipation and excitement hung in the crisp air. For the

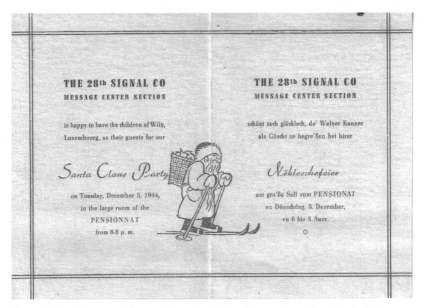

Original Signal Company Message Center invitation. *Courtesy: Oeuvre Saint Nicolas, Wiltz*

townspeople, the party meant a return to the way of life they had enjoyed before the war. They would finally be able to celebrate the holiday season freely and without fear of consequence from the Nazis, beginning—as was the tradition—with Saint Nicolas Day.

For the few soldiers of the signal company message center involved with the party, it was a chance to enjoy the spirit of Christmas, despite not being with their families. Even with the Germans on the run, the war was far from being over; the Keystone Division knew there was no way they'd be home by Christmas, and these few men saw the party as a chance to celebrate as best they could—while they could. After all, Christmas day was still three weeks away. No one knew if or when orders would come, sending the men to who-knows-where by December 25. The occasional distant artillery shell was a harsh reminder that the war was still being fought and not far from Wiltz. The soldiers lived each day with the knowledge that they could be back at the front, in the thick of the fighting, at any time and that each day could be their last. It was an obvious conclusion then that this could also be their last Christmas, and they were determined to make the most of it.

It was well past four o'clock in the afternoon when Corporal Stutz walked into Division HQ looking for Brookins. He spotted him in a small room next to the communications center, cleaning the film projector.

"Hey, St. Nick, are you ready for the festivities?" Stutz called out to Brookins from across the room.

"Very funny," Brookins said acerbically, as he shot Stutz a look of mild displeasure.

"Come on. It's going to be fun. You'll see."

"Fun? I'm not sure this is exactly what I'd call fun, Harry."

"Would you rather be on KP, or even worse—stuck out in the woods freezing your butt off in an observation post? Look, the kids are going to love it, and that's all that matters. Are you about ready to go?"

"Go? Go where?"

"To the castle to get dressed. Father Wolff and some nuns are there waiting for you. They've got his robes and stuff for you."

"Now?" Brookins asked, as he gestured to the gutted film projector sprawled out on the table in front of him.

"Well, yeah," Stutz said. He thrust his left arm out to roll up his sleeve and at the same time glanced at his watch.

"We're looking at sixteen-hundred now. By the time you get to the castle, get dressed and all, it should be pretty close to showtime."

"All right. Just let me put this stuff back together and I'll head up there."

"Okay, but Burton's outside in a jeep waiting for you, so whenever you're ready."

"Tell him to keep the engine running. I'll be out in a second."

Brookins quickly finished cleaning the sprockets of the film projector. A small rubber aspirator like those used in hospital nurseries made an ideal tool for the machine's intricate parts. When Brookins squeezed the soft rubber ball, a burst of air was forced from the narrow cone-shaped tip—gently blowing away dust and lint that found its way into the projector's interior. A soft bristle brush and a clean rag completed the tool set and allowed him to keep the projector relatively clean. Next, he used a piece of linen he'd found to wipe off the glass lens. He would have preferred a piece of lens paper designed specifically for cleaning camera lenses, but there wasn't any around, and he hadn't seen a packet of it—despite requisitioning some—since the trip from England. The projector was also missing its lens cover, so Brookins improvised by draping the piece of linen over the lens like a hood before closing the machine in its travel case. He placed it on the floor with the rest of his equipment and then grabbed his jacket and helmet and hurried outside.

Brookins immediately saw Pvt. Keith Burton, a soldier of average build, black hair, deep-set brown eyes, and an olive-toned round face, sitting behind the wheel of a jeep. He was a couple of years older than Brookins, but most important, he was from Buffalo, New York, not far from Brookins' hometown of Rochester. *And when you're standing in the middle of nowhere*, Burton had remarked when the two first met in basic training, *that's as good as being next-door neighbors.* Burton was a relatively quiet guy, but he and Brookins would often talk about home and places they both knew and, of course, the snow.

"How's it going, Keith? Looks like you're my chauffeur," Brookins said as he climbed into the jeep. "To the castle, James!" he said as he waved his arm around in a circle and pointed forward with a grandiose air.

"Anything you say, Nick," Burton retaliated with a laugh. He pushed down on the clutch, and the jeep jerked into gear.

"Remember, it's *St. N*ick to you, pal!" Brookins countered.

"Yeah? Well I've been around you long enough to know that you ain't no saint. That's for sure!"

From HQ, Burton made a quick U-turn in front of stately house, putting them on the road would take them right up alongside the castle at the north end of town.

Burton slowed at the bend that turned onto the Grand Rue at the town hall but instead made a sharp left onto the cobblestone drive leading through the main portal and into the castle courtyard. He parked the jeep in front of a door that served as the entrance to the convent.

"Door-to-door service," Burton said with a grin as he turned off the engine.

"Now what? Do we wait here? Go in?"

"Dunno. Harry just said to take you to the convent," said Burton nodding at the heavy oak door to their right. "Well, this is it."

Brookins sighed deeply and as the two men got out of the jeep. The heavy wooden door of the convent creaked open, and two nuns stepped out. The nuns looked the men over for a moment and then motioned for them to come inside. The door closed behind them, and a voice greeted them from the dark foyer.

"Hello. I am Father Wolff."

"Hello, Father," the men answered in unison.

"I spoke with Corporal Stutz. It is a wonderful thing you are doing for the children. Who is to be Saint Nicolas?" the priest asked joyfully.

"That's me. I mean, I guess I am," Brookins said.

"I see. And your name?"

"Oh, I'm sorry." Brookins said removing his helmet and extending his hand. "Brookins. Corporal Richard Brookins, and this is Keith Burton. He drove the jeep."

"How's it going, Father?" Burton said as he removed his helmet and shook the priest's hand. "Oh, I almost forgot!" he said and then turned and darted out of the foyer, leaving Brookins and the others standing in uncomfortable silence. Brookins blew into his hands and rubbed them together to warm them as he smiled nervously at the nuns and Father Wolff.

"A little cold today," he said, trying to think of the German word for cold. The word was on the tip of his tongue when the door to the foyer swung open, breaking the uneasy silence, and a slightly winded Keith Burton stepped into the room.

"Sorry, Father. Corporal Stutz told me to give you this for the church." Burton handed a new army-issued broom to the priest.

Father Wolff smiled and nodded as he accepted the gift.

"I must thank him. It is very kind," the priest said as he inspected the broom.

"What's that all about?" a confused Brookins whispered aside to Burton.

"Beats me. Harry just told me to make sure the priest got it. I guess he needed a broom."

Father Wolff then spoke to the nuns in Lëtzebuergesch. The nuns smiled and bowed slightly towards Brookins and Burton. It was obvious that the two men had just been introduced, so Brookins smiled and gave a little wave towards the nuns, and Burton mimicked him.

"Well, if you are ready, the sisters and I will help you with the robes," Father Wolff said, motioning to a room off the foyer.

"Oh, sure. Ready as I'll ever be."

"I'll just wait here," Burton said, smirking and pointing at one of the large, ornately carved chairs in the foyer.

"Coward," Brookins taunted over his shoulder as he followed Father Wolff and the nuns into the next room.

"Everything is here," Father Wolff said as he motioned to the table in the center of the room. On the table was a long white priest's cassock trimmed in lace, an outer cape made of heavy wool and adorned with gold stars and gold braid edging, a bishop's miter, a pair of white cloth gloves, and something that looked like a pile of frayed rope.

"The sisters will help you with everything. They have been preparing," the priest said, lightly touching the newly hand-sewn gold stars. "I must tend to some things, and then I will meet you when you are ready."

"Okay. Thanks, Father," Brookins said as the priest bowed slightly and left the room.

Brookins suddenly realized that with Father Wolff gone, no one in the room could communicate with him. The nuns hadn't spoken and didn't seem to understand English, and he certainly didn't understand their language. However, he had managed to pick up some German since he'd been on the continent, and between that, what he knew from high school and some miming, the three were able to get him ready.

Brookins donned the priest's white cassock over his uniform. It came in two parts, both of which were made of very light linen. The first piece, worn as a foundation garment, was unremarkable, while the second robe was a bit shorter than the first and more elaborately decorated with red and gold fabric and a light lace trim in front. The nuns helped Brookins with the heavy wool outer cape, draping it over his head like a poncho. The cape was only about waist high in the front, but it was long and trailed after him in back.

Once Brookins was properly dressed, one of the nuns picked-up the pile of frayed rope and handed it to him. Brookins quickly realized that the lumpy rope was to be his "beard." *Of course,* he thought to himself, *what would Santa Claus or St. Nick be without a white beard?* The nuns secured the rope beard in place with a ribbon tied behind Brookins' head. The beard hung from just beneath Brookins' nose down to his chest, and there was a hole cut in it for his mouth.

Next came the bishop's miter. The nuns tried to place it on top of Brookins' head but it was too small and wouldn't stay in place. After several attempts to push the hat onto his head, Brookins took the hat from them and gently pulled at the headband, stretching it as much as he could without tearing it. Finally, after a few minutes and a few more attempts by the sisters to force the hat onto Brookins' head, the hat had stretched enough for him to wear it. It was tight, very tight, but it was as loose as it was going to get without ripping.

Brookins was just about finished when the door opened and Father Wolff ushered in two girls who looked to be about eight or nine years old.

"What would Saint Nicolas be without his *Engelcher?*" the priest said, but then he paused as he tried to remember the words in English. "Little angels. We have little angels for you. They are from the school here, at the top of their class. This is Liliane Wampach, and she is Jeanny Schleimer. They will be your help."

The girls wore white dresses with white socks and shoes, and attached to each of their dresses was a pair of cloth angel's wings held in place with white ribbon and tied in front with a bow. The girls also wore white ribbons meant to look like halos around their heads. Their gazes were fixed on the tall man standing before them. Brookins smiled at them but said nothing, knowing that they wouldn't understand him anyway.

One of the nuns walked over and picked up a crozier, a sort of shepherd's staff that had been broken and joined together with tape. It had been leaning against the wall and she offered it to Brookins. He quickly pulled on the white cloth gloves and took the crozier from the nun.

"Shall we go?" Father Wolff asked.

Brookins examined the crozier for a moment and then nodded to Father Wolff. The two girls left the room first, followed by Brookins and the nuns. As Brookins stepped into the foyer, Burton got up from the chair he had been sitting in and smiled broadly.

"Not a word," Brookins commanded pointing the crozier at Burton.

"Saint Nicolas, I presume?" Burton teased.

"You're lucky these kids are here or I'd break this stick over your head."

"Well, the day is still young. I'd better get my helmet on just in case," Burton said as he opened the door to the courtyard. He ran around to the driver's side of the jeep, jumped in, and started the motor.

Brookins strolled to the jeep and began climbing in but stopped abruptly and leaned the crozier against the vehicle. He bent down, picked up the girls one at a time and placed them in the back seat of the jeep. Then he grabbed the crozier and got into the jeep next to Burton.

"What are you doing?" asked Burton, an eyebrow raised, an indignant look feigned at Brookins.

"What?"

"Look, if I'm gonna be driving around with Saint Nicolas, he'd better be in the back with his angels, not sitting up front with some dogface," Burton said motioning for Brookins to get in the back.

Brookins realized that Burton was right. He signed heavily then clambered into the back seat between the two girls, being careful not to catch the robes on anything that might tear them. Burton was about to put the jeep into gear when Father Wolff held up his hand.

"Something wrong, Father?" Burton asked.

Father Wolff shook his head and smiled as he looked over the jeep and its passengers.

"May God and the spirit of Saint Nicolas be with you," he said as he made the sign of the cross over the jeep and then stepped back.

Burton nodded his thanks to the priest, threw a quick glance back towards Saint Nicolas and his angels, and then put the jeep in gear. He spun it around the castle courtyard and then drove through the portal and out along the cobbled drive.

CHAPTER 8

Cpl. Morton Hale and Pvt. First Class Vincent LaCosta spent most of their morning filming soldiers of the 9th Infantry Division as they moved into Losheim, Germany, and now under a clear late-afternoon sky, they perched on a bluff overlooking the Roer River. From there they had a sweeping vista of the valley and a clear view across the river into Germany. Peering through binoculars, Hale could see German soldiers far across the river; small squads marching in formation along narrow roads, going somewhere with some purpose; manning and maintaining battery positions and gun emplacements along their side of the river; off-loading supply trucks; doing any of the numerous daily routines an army does while it waits and prepares—for what? Spying the soldiers, Hale couldn't help but crack a wry smile, knowing their future. He continued scanning the river valley when just past four o'clock, the low drone of engines echoed up the ridge.

"There," he said pointing the binoculars down river. "About three o'clock. Coming in low."

LaCosta also heard the engines and sprang into action, swinging his tripod-mounted 16-mm Bell & Howell 70 camera to the direction where Hale was pointing. Through the viewfinder, LaCosta quickly acquired his target: three Army Air Force Douglas A-20 bombers flying in formation up the river valley. He panned the camera, tracking their flight path as they made their bombing run at their German targets. Moments later, explosions ripped along the far side of the river. The ground beneath his feet shook, but LaCosta kept the camera steady, focusing on the aftermath.

Rolls of yellow-orange flame churned through curls of thickening black smoke pouring from the opposite river bank. Through his binoculars, Hale soaked in the devastation.

"You get all that?" he asked.

"You know I did," LaCosta replied, his eye still pressed to the camera.

The planes continued on and out of sight as Hale and LaCosta, having gotten what they came for, packed up their gear, turned their jeep around, and headed back toward Wiltz.

At the public school near the center of town, the celebration was already underway. The children, along with mothers, sisters, young brothers, grandparents, and aunts all gathered outside awaiting the arrival of Saint Nicolas. The children, some wearing costumes and led by the teachers, sang songs and danced, or recited poems in honor of the good saint. One of the GIs from the signal company, Hank Fiebig, had a guitar and managed to strum along to their songs. However, when the singing stopped, Hank would continue the music with his rendition of Jingle Bells, singing the verses over and over; it was the only holiday song he knew.

Noticeably absent from the festivities were most of the fathers, uncles, and older brothers. Some had been taken by the Nazis and conscripted into the German army or forced to work in the labor camps. Some had been sent to concentration camps for refusing to help the Germans. Some, who were on the Gestapo's "most wanted" list, remained in hiding, awaiting the end of the war. Still others remained here in Wiltz, buried in a cemetery several hundred yards away.

Private Burton slowed the jeep as he approached the semicircle of people gathered in front of the school. The singing died away, and the children's faces lit with excitement as the jeep neared and everyone could finally see who was sitting in the back. Burton pulled the jeep to a stop just in front of the group.

"Curbside service, St. Nick. Should I keep the meter running?" he quipped.

Brookins chuckled a bit but said nothing; he was too nervous to speak. *"There's nothing to it. A pat on the head, a pinch on the cheek." That's what Harry said a few days ago when I agreed to this,* Brookins thought. It had sounded easy enough at the time, but this—this was more than he had expected. Brookins looked over the crowd and quickly estimated that there were at least sixty children—sixty pairs of eager, awestruck eyes staring back at him. And then there were the parents, beaming joyfully

at Saint Nicolas as their children reveled in the festivities. It was overwhelming. He reached into his pocket and pulled out a package of gum. The white gloves made it difficult to take a stick out of the pack and pull off the wrapper, but a few moments of fidgeting freed the gum, and he quickly shoved it through the rope beard into his mouth. He gestured to his two angels with the package of gum, but the girls said nothing.

"Gum?" Brookins said again gesturing with the pack. Still

Above: "The American St. Nick" with his angels arriving at the Wiltz castle on December 5, 1944. (Harry Stutz is the third soldier standing from the left, partially obscured.) *Photo: National Archives*

Below: "The American St. Nick" with "Black Peter" and the angels Liliane Wampach and Jeanny Schleimer. Henry "Hank" Fiebig sings and plays guitar. December 5, 1944. *Photo: National Archives*

the girls said nothing, but smiled and shook their heads.

"Sure?" Brookins asked before realizing that they probably didn't understand him. *What's the word for gum?*

"Uh, they're waiting for you, St. Nick," Burton interrupted.

"All right, all right. Take it easy," Brookins answered. He climbed over

"The American St. Nick" arrives at the public school with "Black Peter" (Jemp Bettel), December 5, 1944. *Photo: National Archives*

the front seat and stepped out, jerking noticeably when startled by the children breaking into song again. He started moving toward the group before remembering that he had left the two little girls in the jeep. He turned back and was surprised to see that the angels had not only climbed out of the jeep on their own, but they were also dutifully holding the train of his robe, being careful not to let it drag on the ground. Brookins smiled nervously at the two girls and nodded in appreciation, realizing that the nuns at the convent must have instructed them. He continued toward the singing children, nervousness preventing him from noticing the *Stars and Stripes* photographer taking pictures. He also didn't notice the two combat cameramen, Hale and LaCosta, who had arrived into town in time to see something amazing: a jeep with what looked like Santa Claus riding in the back, exiting the castle and passing right in front of them. Curiosity had gotten the better of them and Hale followed, bringing their jeep to a stop at the school as well. LaCosta grabbed his camera and quickly checked to see how much film he had left while Hale wrote out a quick slate on a small chalkboard. A few seconds later, the camera whirred, and LaCosta walked about, eye pressed to the viewfinder.

As Brookins timidly approached the children, they sang along with the strumming guitar but kept their eyes fixed on him, watching his every move. Brookins could read the excitement and disbelief on their faces as Saint Nicolas walked amongst them—something they had waited for and wished for longer than some of them could remember. The song ended, and everyone applauded. As if on cue, Harvey Hamann and Ben Kimmelman (a captain from the company's dental unit) arrived, carrying a tray of doughnuts and candy between them.

"Come and get 'em," they called, but none of the children moved. Their awe-filled eyes fixed on Saint Nicolas, continuing to watch his every move.

"Doughnuts and candy. Come and get 'em," Hamann repeated, his voice raised slightly in case the children hadn't heard him the first time, but still none of the children stepped forward, even at the urging of their parents. Hamann and Kimmelman looked around at the crowd and then at each other, wondering why no one wanted the treats.

"Come on," Kimmelman smiled to the children as he motioned with his free arm, "Fresh doughnuts and chocolate. They're good," he said rubbing his stomach.

"Maybe if Saint Nicolas passed out a few?" Hamann suggested.

Brookins nodded, grabbed a couple of doughnuts, and then turned and smiled, handing them to the child closest to him. The little boy's face glowed with excitement as he took the treats from Saint Nicolas. Brookins thought for a moment, trying to remember the words as he bent down closer to the boy.

"What's your name?" he asked in German, one of a handful of phrases he remembered from a high school German language class. It was all that was needed. The smile on the boy's face grew bright with delight. Saint Nicolas was speaking to *him*. The boy said something, but Brookins didn't understand him. He just smiled and patted the boy on the head, and suddenly, for the first time since he'd gotten out of the jeep, Brookins wasn't nervous anymore.

He stood up, and the semicircle quickly closed in around him. Likewise, Hamann and Kimmelman were suddenly besieged with children. They tried to pass out the donuts and candy as fast as they could but were unable to keep up with the stream of eager hands. Harry saw the crush of children and stood with Hamann and Kimmelman trying to help, but it was no use. Their situation hopeless, the soldiers were forced to surrender by simply holding onto the tray and making sure it didn't tip over while the children helped themselves to the treats. Meanwhile Saint

Nicolas continued through the crowd, meeting the children and handing out candy.

The atmosphere in the square was light and festive; the children, their parents, the nuns, and the GIs were all genuinely enjoying themselves. It had been so long since Wiltz had had the means or the opportunity to celebrate that lifting the peoples' spirits was a simple task. Wiltz had been spared the destruction brought on by the war, but it had suffered greatly from the depravity that war brings. To a people that had nothing left, the simplicity of this small holiday party with its songs and dances, treats and candies, and the presence of Saint Nicolas himself was all that was needed to revive the joy and essence of the season. The GIs were rewarded as well. After hearing the reasons behind the Saint Nicolas Day celebration, the men of the 28th Division Signal Company Message Center had happily donated not only the candy from their rations but also gifts and packages from home. Such open charity lifted their own spirits and overshadowed the disappointment of being so far from home.

For the next forty minutes or so, Saint Nicolas circulated amongst the children, asking their names and passing out treats. He was careful to make sure that he stopped to meet every child who was in the square, and he and the other GIs made sure each child received some sort of Christmas treat. Then it was time to head back to the castle, where there would be more children waiting.

Saint Nicolas and his angels climbed back into the jeep and the crowd formed a procession to follow them to the castle. Burton drove as slowly as he could without stalling the jeep, trying not to outdistance the crowd. All along the main street, young and old alike waved as the jeep passed, eager to get Saint Nicolas' attention. Wiltz had come alive.

Once at the castle, Burton again drove into the courtyard, where the remaining children had assembled. The children were surprised not only at seeing Saint Nicolas riding in the back of a jeep but also by receiving his blessing. Brookins didn't realize he was making the sign of the cross. It hadn't been something he'd planned on doing, but after spending the past forty minutes or so with the other children, his nervousness had abated, and he had fallen wholeheartedly into his role. The spirit of the moment had seized him, and before he could stop himself, his right hand was gesturing the sign of the cross over the crowd as the jeep cleared the portal.

Burton parked the jeep, and once again, Saint Nicolas climbed down, his angels dutifully following behind. He confidently walked up to where

an ornate red carpet had been placed on the ground. Around the edges of the carpet stood seventeen little girls, all dressed like angels, and each holding a small flag of Luxembourg. Behind the girls, all the other children stood waiting. As he approached, the angels began singing a song to honor his arrival, and soon the rest of the crowd joined in. Brookins

Above: Courtyard of the Wiltz castle, December 5, 1944. *Photo: Richard Brookins*

Below: Children holding flags of Luxembourg and singing to honor "The American St. Nick" in the courtyard of the Wiltz castle, December 5, 1944. *Photo: National Archives*

stood at the end of the carpet, smiling and nodding as the children sang.

When they finished, one of the nuns from the convent stepped forward and addressed the group. Brookins didn't understand what she was saying, but as soon as she finished, she approached him and motioned toward one of the castle doors. Brookins walked slowly toward the door as the crowd began singing another song. He turned and gestured with the crozier and nodded in appreciation, knowing that they were once again singing a song to Saint Nicolas.

Richard Brookins, "The American St. Nick," in the Wiltz castle, December 5, 1944. Harry Stutz is the soldier on the very left edge of the frame with "Maisy" on his knee. *Photo: Oeuvre Saint Nicolas, Wiltz*

Brookins was led into a large room just off the courtyard and seated in a large chair. He sat holding the crozier in his white-gloved hand, with his two angels standing on either side of him as the crowd made their way into the room. GIs from "the Christmas Committee" stood behind tables, handing out treats. At another table, two nuns from the convent were passing out cups of hot chocolate. When all the children had found a place in the great room, one of the nuns announced a series of songs, dances, and skits, all designed to honor and entertain Saint Nicolas. As the children performed, Brookins and the other soldiers' hearts soared, and their faces beamed with delight. There was little doubt in anyone's mind that this was the best Saint Nicolas Day celebration these children had had in years.

After the performances, the children lined up to meet and talk to Saint Nicolas. One by one, they would sit on his knee and tell him what they wished for on Saint Nicolas Day. Brookins didn't always understand what the children were saying, but he didn't need to. In German he would ask their names and then wait for them to respond. Then he would smile and nod as if he understood every word they were saying. Occasionally, he would hear the German word for *mother* or *father*, and Brookins would nod and repeat the word, helping the children to believe that he indeed knew what they were saying. After listening to their Saint Nicolas Day wishes, he would kiss them on the cheek or forehead or give them a pat on the head, and they would be on their way as the next child approached. The procession had continued uninterrupted for almost an hour when Harry walked up to Saint Nicolas' throne. Harry waited for Saint Nicolas to finish his audience with a little boy and then quickly approached before the next child came forward.

"How's it going, St. Nick?"

"It's going pretty good. I don't know how I ever let you talk me into this, Harry, but I'm glad you did."

"See! I told you it'd be fun and easy."

"I know. You were right, and these kids are great. Have you seen their faces? They're having a ball!"

"Yeah, well, it seems to me that St. Nick is too! Can I get you anything? Are you thirsty? Want some coffee or hot chocolate or something?" Stutz offered.

"No, but thanks anyway. To tell you the truth, I don't think I could keep anything down if I tried," Brookins said with his tone turning serious.

"What's the matter? You can't still be nervous. You're doing great! The kids love it."

"No, it's not that, it's this hat. It's too tight! I've got a headache like you read about," Brookins quietly explained to Stutz.

"You'd never know it by the way you're carrying on with these kids. Have you tried stretching it out?"

"Of course. That was the first thing I did. I was able to loosen it up a bit, but I guess after wearing it for a while, sweating and all, it must have tightened up or something. It's killing me!"

"Well, then take it off. No sense making yourself sick over it. Here, let me . . ." Stutz reached for bishop's miter.

"No, don't!" Brookins exclaimed putting his hand up to stop Stutz. "Leave it alone."

"Look, Brooks . . ."

"No, leave it alone. I'll be all right."

"But if your head's pounding . . ."

"No. I don't want to take it off yet. If I take it off now, I don't know,

67

it might ruin the whole Saint Nicolas thing for these kids. I can wait a while longer."

Stutz studied Brookins for a moment, without saying a word. He looked at the children waiting in line, and the people crowding the room. Everyone was smiling and laughing. Some of the children were playing games or singing, while others were enjoying their hot chocolate and candy gifts. Stutz turned back to Brookins and smiled.

"You're right, St. Nick. I know exactly what you mean. Keep it up, you're doing great!"

"Thanks," Brookins said as Stutz turned and walked away from the throne. Brookins continued to visit with the children. Finally, after the last child had talked with Saint Nicolas, the Mother Superior of the convent approached.

"Thank you for everything," she said though a heavy accent, as she took Brookins' hand in hers.

"Oh, you're welcome," Brookins replied politely.

"You and the others have been most generous. The children—they are very happy. This they will remember always, as will we." She looked into Brookins' eyes and squeezed his hand.

Brookins smiled at her, unsure of how to react to what she had just said, or more precisely, the *way* she said it.

"Yes, well, it was fun. It was good for us too. We're very happy," he finally stammered.

"I am sorry, but it is time. The Father—he will need the robes for the Mass." She motioned to a door behind the chair where Brookins was sitting.

Brookins looked at the door and then back at Mother Superior; it took him a moment to understand what she meant.

"Oh, of course," he said, quickly getting to his feet and starting for the door. The Mother Superior caught his arm.

"One moment, please," she said to him and then faced the crowd. She clapped her hands to get people's attention and then spoke to them in Lëtzebuergesch. A few moments later the children broke into another song. Brookins listened, although he didn't understand the words, and he waved to everyone in the room. After about a minute, he saw the Mother Superior gesture to the door once again. Brookins again started to the door but stopped abruptly, turning to his two angels who had stood by his side the entire time. He bent down and kissed each of the girls on the forehead and gave them a pat on the cheek.

"Thank you," he said to each of them in German, as he cupped their faces in his white-gloved hands. The two girls smiled back at Saint Nicolas, their faces registering pure delight. Then Brookins turned and headed for the door. He paused in the doorway and scanned the crowd, quickly locating Harry off to one side. Harry smiled broadly, waved at Saint Nicolas and gave him a thumbs-up. Brookins smiled back and raised his right hand to his forehead in a casual salute to his friend. Saint Nicolas then turned and left the room.

Brookins was surprised to find himself back in the room where he had donned the priest's robes a few hours earlier. He wasn't sure how all the rooms were connected in the castle, but somehow he was back where he had started. He let the door close behind him and then quickly removed the bishop's miter from his head. He could feel the pulse of blood rushing back into his scalp, and the indentation the hat's band had made in his skin.

"Oh, that's better," he signed loudly as the cool castle air seized his creased, sweaty brow. The nuns who were in the room to collect the robes didn't know what Brookins had said, but as they watched him drop into another large wooden chair and rub the life back into his temples and scalp, they understood.

Brookins removed the white gloves and rope beard; the chilly air was just as refreshing on his sweaty hands and face as it had been on his head. He leaned back in the chair and let his head rest against the cool castle wall for a few moments; the crisp air showering over him. Then, in one deft motion, he stood and slipped all the robes over his head and handed them to one of the nuns. The other nun approached and placed a basin of warm water and a towel on the table next to Brookins. He splashed water onto his face and then buried it in the soft towel. He ran his fingers through his hair, smoothing it. He straightened his uniform as best he could and once again collapsed back down in the chair and leaned his head against the wall. His mind wandered, taking in the day's events, while singing children finished their song to Saint Nicolas. Clapping and laughter followed, and the party continued. Still resting his head against the wall, he closed his eyes, realizing the pounding headache was gone and he was smiling.

CHAPTER 9

The days following the Christmas party were filled with routine tasks. The message center unit spent its time relaying messages or doing other tedious chores that needed to be done while the division was in stand-down mode. Supplies and reinforcements continued to stream into Wiltz. The soldiers knew that when the Keystone Division was on its feet again, they would be pressed back into service, only this time they hoped the fight would take them into the heart of Germany and maybe even to Berlin and the end of the war in Europe.

For the people of Wiltz, the days following the Saint Nicolas Day celebrations meant a return to normalcy, or as close as they could come given the circumstances. The children returned to school, parents returned to their jobs, and thanks mostly to the soldiers of the message center, everyone began looking forward to Christmas, which was only a couple of weeks away.

Brookins spent most of his days at headquarters bent over his highly classified SIGABA cryptography machine. Resembling a bulky typewriter, the SIGABA featured a full keyboard at the front with three sets of five rotors inside that coded and decoded messages as the operator typed. The SIGABA was also motor-driven, allowing it to print out coded messages on small strips of paper.

When he finished his duty and left Villa Adler for the day, Brookins half-expected someone from town to stop and talk to him or thank him for being Saint Nicolas, but no one ever did. After more than a week, Brookins finally realized the reason—no one from the town knew he was

Saint Nicolas. The costume, as primitive as it was, concealed his identity so thoroughly that none of the children knew it was an American soldier pretending to be Saint Nicolas. When Brookins had donned the robes and later in the day taken them off, no one was around except Father Wolff and the two nuns who had helped him. As far as the children were concerned, it was Saint Nicolas in the castle that day.

At two in the afternoon on Friday, December 15, Sgt. Frank Teterus, Brookins' section leader, told him that at the end of his duty that day, he would be assigned temporary duty (TD) with the 110th Regiment up in Clervaux.

"They want you to show movies to the guys up there," Teterus said. "When you get there, report to a Lieutenant Thompson. He knows you're coming. They'll assign you a place to stay when you get there."

"Sure thing, Sarg," Brookins said dutifully. "Any idea how long I'm gonna be up there on TD?"

"Can't say for sure, so make sure you get your mail forwarded there. We'll get you back here ASAP, but for now, just get things squared away up there. Remember: Lieutenant Thompson. Got it?"

"Thompson. Got it," Brookins answered.

"As soon as you're done, grab your gear and head up there. I've got a jeep outside with all your movie equipment already loaded up. Check it to make sure it's all there."

After his shift ended, Brookins collected most of his personal belongings at the Hotel Bellevue, including his .30-caliber M-1 carbine, and hustled back down to HQ and the waiting jeep.

"You Brookins?" the driver asked.

"That'd be me," Brookins said while scanning the equipment stashed in the back.

"Let's hit it. I wanna get back before it gets dark. I hate driving these roads in the dark. It's slippery as all get-out, and ya can't see for love or money," the driver said as he cranked the engine.

"Just let me make sure everything's here. I don't know who loaded this stuff, but I don't want to be missing anything when we get there," Brookins replied. Everything he needed appeared to be there: the two 16-mm film projectors, a portable screen, voltage transformer, and three film reels containing the movie *Going My Way*. He put his gear in the back with the film equipment—everything but the M-1. That he held onto as he climbed into the jeep.

"All right. Let's go," he finally said.

The driver threw it into gear, and the jeep lurched forward, speeding them past the public school and winding through the outskirts of town towards Clervaux, only fifteen miles to the north.

Despite clear evening skies, the weather remained cold and damp and the drive along the muddy, rutted, and in some places icy, narrow roads snaking through the Ardennes hills made the trip much longer than had been expected. More than an hour later, in rapidly fading daylight, the jeep turned onto the main road into Clervaux at the northern end of town. Driving along the street, they passed the train station on their left and moments later on their right as the driver pointed out the Hotel Claravallis, headquarters for the 110th Regiment. Making their way onto the Grand Rue in the heart of the old-world town, it was easy to see why command chose this spot for R & R. Tucked along the banks of the Clerve River, beneath steep, lush forested ravines, Clervaux had been an idyllic vacation retreat before the war. With quaint buildings lining hilly, winding, cobblestone streets, it was the perfect spot for GIs to take a break from the war. The soldiers came in on three-day rotations and enjoyed the luxury of hot showers and hot food, comfortable beds, clean clothing, and plenty of recreational activities and entertainment, which included seeing Hollywood movies. They drove into a small square at the other end of town where the driver brought the jeep to a stop in front of the Central Hotel. Brookins was immediately awestruck by an enormous castle perched on the crest of a bluff a short distance behind the hotel. Built on ancient foundations, construction of the castle began in the 12th century and continued through the centuries with various additions and renovations. It was Frederic the First who commissioned the massive Burgundy tower housing the castle jail, and sometime later, the castle's defenses were improved with the addition of the imposing tower in the main courtyard.

"Impressive, huh?" the driver said, elbowing Brookins.

"I'll say."

"C'mon. I'll help ya unload this stuff. Then I gotta get back," the driver said climbing out of the jeep.

The Central Hotel was the administration and R & R hub for the 110th, with a mess hall, lounge, and game room. The two men unloaded the equipment from the jeep and brought it into the hotel, placing it against a wall just inside the game room. As soon as all the equipment was in, the driver unceremoniously hopped back into the jeep, threw Brookins a wave, and headed back to Wiltz. Brookins looked around the lobby of the hotel, asked a soldier who seemed like he knew the lay of the land and who in fact did know where to find Lieutenant Thompson, pointing at the officer standing at the far end of the room.

"Right. The movie guy," Thompson said, scanning the presented orders. "Sergeant, this is Brookins," he said to the soldier standing to his right. "He's been assigned here on TD. He's got movies to show to the men. Let's see what we can do about getting him squared away with a room and rations. Why don't you get settled, grab some chow, and meet me down here tomorrow at 0900 with some sort of schedule for showing films to the men."

After getting his room assignment in the hotel, Brookins left all his gear where they'd stacked it and as the Lieutenant suggested went into the mess hall on the main floor of the Central for a leisurely dinner and smoke. He'd thought about visiting one of the many pubs in the town where, despite the war, beer and wine—albeit watered down—was readily available for thirsty GIs on leave. However, after being on duty all day at Villa Adler and then the drive up, fatigue was taking hold, and he had a schedule to work out before the morning. Instead, Brookins grabbed his duffle bag and rifle and went up to his room and the promise of clean sheets and a good night's sleep. He swung open the door to his room and was greeted by a snappy, bright-eyed "Hi!" from a soldier sitting cross-legged on a bed against the wall opposite the door.

"Eugene Harrington," the soldier said, putting down a notepad and pen and extending his hand.

"Brookins, Richard Brookins. I guess we're roommates," he said shaking Hugh's hand and nodding at the notepad. "Everyone just sort of calls me Brooks. Don't let me interrupt the letter home."

"It's actually a journal. Sort of diary, I guess, but I ain't got much to write about. I ain't seen any action since I've been over here. And everyone just calls me Hugh. I got my name from my grandfather on my dad's side who lives with us," Hugh explained while Brookins stowed his gear and settled into the room. "The problem is ya can't have two Eugenes sitting at the dinner table. It's gets confusing when someone says 'Eugene, please pass the salt' and we both reach for it. Besides, everyone in town knows my granddad as Gene, so for me they just shortened it to Hugh."

"Makes sense," Brookins said. "Hugh it is."

Brookins sat on the other bed in the room, pulled out his cigarettes, and offered one to Hugh who accepted and wedged it behind his ear.

"For later," Hugh said, nodding and smiling his thanks while Brookins plugged one into the corner of his mouth. For the next couple of hours, they talked, getting to know each other. Younger than Brookins, Hugh Harrington—with his slick brown hair, toothy smile, and movie magazine looks—was born and raised in the small farming community of Crow Wing, Minnesota. His father worked the farm while his mother was the consummate housewife, raising him and his three brothers and a sister. Working on the family farm since before he could remember, Hugh was always more mechanically inclined, with school and academics holding little interest. He wanted to enlist in the army on his eighteenth birthday primarily as a way of seeing a world he knew only from history books, newspapers, and (since the beginning of the war) on the radio. His birthday, however, was at the end of June, and his parents, who didn't want him enlisting in the first place, made him promise not to join the fighting until he graduated high school a year later in June of 1943. By that time, his parents hoped, the war would over at best or at least ending shortly. That summer, however, Hugh's father fell ill, forcing Hugh to remain home and help with the farm until his father was well enough to work. It was in February 1944 that Hugh finally enlisted in the army at Fort Snelling, volunteering for tank duty. By that time, however, the army was in desperate need of replacements, and following basic training, Hugh was assigned to the 112th Regiment of the 28th Infantry Division. By October 1944, he was in Luxembourg, although his assignments kept him away from combat to perform necessary but routine "grunt" work.

"One time I got picked to go out on this patrol, which I think really meant 'go out and see if there are any stray Germans hanging around,'" Hugh recalled enthusiastically. "So we go out, passing through all these tiny towns where there is nothing but dairy farms—at least they looked like the dairy farms we have back home, except there were no cows or nothing because the Germans took everything that wasn't nailed down. So there were just these open fields as far as you could see. We kept going, figuring there ain't no Germans around because where would they be hiding, it being so open and such. Anyway we went into this one town, I don't remember the name, but there wasn't nothing in this town but a handful of houses, a few barns, and a church, and they're all on this one road because it's the only road in and out of town. Now the road, well it sort of winds through the town in sort of an S shape," Hugh traced on his blanket with his finger. "Now, on one of the corners of the S on our left is the church," Hugh pointed at the ripple he'd just created. "So we slowed down to check out the church and such, and as we rounded the bend, about a hundred yards away, coming right at us around the other bend in the S, is a German staff car," Hugh said, his eyes again wide with excitement. "Well they saw us and hit the brakes, and we hit the brakes, and now we're looking at them and they're looking at us, and no one's moving because I think we were all in shock or something." Hugh was laughing now, as was Brookins. "Anyway, I'm in sitting in the jeep, green as grass thinking all hell's about to break loose when all of a sudden the Krauts revved up, spun that car around, and high-tailed out of there as fast as they could go."

"So what did you guys do?" said Brookins laughing in amazement.

"Well, we just sat there for few seconds looking at each other, sort of like 'did you just see what I saw?' and without saying a word, Murphy, the guy driving, turns us around and hits the gas. We laughed all the way back to HQ, and all I could picture in my head was those Germans high-tailing it out of one end of town and us going like bats-out-of-hell out of the other!"

The two laughed as Brookins lit another cigarette and then offered his still flaming Zippo to Hugh for his 'for later.'

"But the thing is, that's the only action I've seen since I've been here. Now they put me on R & R! What do I need with R & R? I didn't even bring my rifle. They said I wouldn't be needing it. It doesn't make any sense to me, but if the army says you're going on R & R . . . well, who am I to argue?" Hugh shrugged.

Brookins laughed, took a deep drag on his cigarette, watched the exhaled smoke drift across the room, and began sharing some of his own history. He'd been born and raised in Rochester, New York. His father drove a delivery truck for the Wonder Bread company while is mother was a housewife. Brookins spoke of his fiancée, Virginia, who he had met during his last year of high school. He graduated in 1939, but after meeting Virginia decided to go back to school for a post-graduate term to be with her for her senior year. She graduated a year later. Following high school, he had several part-time jobs, including drug store clerk and soda jerk.

"I was well qualified to be a jerk," he joked, getting another toothy laugh out of Hugh. Brookins then landed a job as an expeditor with Ritter

Dental Manufacturing. Although the company manufactured dental and medical equipment, when war broke out, they secured a lend-lease contract with the government, and after some minor factory retooling, began making aviation control column assemblies for British fighter planes and bombers. Brookins worked there for nearly two years, anticipating his draft notice until December 1942, when he decided he'd waited enough and enlisted in the army. During basic training, he was chosen to attend classes and learn how to use the army's top-secret cryptography equipment: the SIGABA. He was later given the rank of corporal and assigned to the 28th Infantry Division in the Signal Company Message Center as a radio operator, cryptographer, and projectionist. Once in England for overseas training, Brookins went from unit to unit, showing the men training films and Hollywood releases ahead of their deployment into France.

The two smoked and talked for the next few hours, reminiscing about home, about the girls they'd left behind, their parents, their towns, favorite teams and sports, what they did before the war, and what they hoped to do after. They spoke about the upcoming Christmas holiday and how they would have celebrated had they been home. They talked about their favorite Christmases past, presents they'd received and given, family traditions, favorite songs, favorite treats, and Christmas dinners. Once on the topic of food, they talked about all the things they missed eating since coming overseas and agreed the one thing they missed the most was butter.

It was nearly ten o'clock when the soldiers, now fast friends, decided to call it a night.

"By the way, what's the movie?" asked Hugh.

"As a matter of fact, it's a Christmas movie . . ."

CHAPTER 10

It was just past five in the morning when Brookins and Harrington were shaken out of their sleep by what sounded like thunder. It took a moment for all of their senses to fully awaken. A much louder rumble struck, and they realized that the thunder was actually artillery shells exploding in the town. They saw a bright flash like lightning followed a moment later by another explosion that shook the hotel and rattled the windows as the shell hit its target. Both men jumped out of bed and foolishly, without thinking of exploding shells and shattering glass, stole a look out of their window. The glow of fires on the low, misty sky was casting an eerie light over Clervaux, and although they could see no one in the street below, they could hear the distinctive squeaking and grinding sound of tank traffic coming from a road high on the ridge across from the hotel. Not sure what was happening, they immediately began grabbing their gear when they heard the shrill whistle of another shell approaching.

"Down!" Brookins yelled as the two men dove to the floor and rolled under the beds as far as they could fit. The whistling sound faded for just a moment before the shell exploded just down the street from the hotel. The window glass shattered, showering the two men with its shards.

"That was too close!" Hugh yelled through the dust and bits of ceiling debris raining down on them.

"What's going on?" Brookins asked out loud. He suspected he knew exactly what was happening, but he still hoped he was wrong. If the Germans were firing artillery into the town ahead of what sounded like tank traffic coming from over the ridge, it probably meant German armor might soon be coming down the road into town, followed by infantry. But considering the latest intelligence reports that Brookins knew of, that simply could not be happening; the Germans were supposed to be strengthening their defenses, not going on the attack.

"Let's get out of here and find out what's happening," Brookins said and the two men jumped to their feet, dusted off the bits of glass, and quickly gathered their things.

Hugh opened the door, and the two men ran down the hall to the stairway that was already clogged with GIs scrambling and yelling, trying to get to their posts or trying to get somewhere for cover. In the lobby, Lieutenant Thompson was already herding the GIs into small groups. Communications with HQ on the other side of town were cut, and no one seemed to know what was happening and what to do next. Thompson acted quickly, sending groups in various directions as scouts to get a sense of the enemy strengths and positions, make contact with forward outposts if possible and to engage the Germans if necessary. He finally turned his attention to Brookins and Harrington.

"Here's what I need from you two," Thompson began. "We've lost contact with HQ. You guys are now runners for the message center until we can get the lines back up. Get up there, report on what's happening here and wait for further orders. Got it?"

"Yes, sir," they responded and then turned heel and headed out the door. Of the two, only Brookins carried a weapon, his M-1 carbine, so he took the lead as they began weaving through Clervaux in an attempt to get to HQ on the other side of town. A freezing mist hung in the cold morning air as mortar shells continued falling all over town. Everywhere soldiers ran chaotically through the streets on the way to their assigned positions while trying to avoid explosions and burning buildings.

"Hey, Brooks, how come they want us both to be runners?" Hugh quizzed as they sprinted through GI clogged streets. "I mean I know you're a signal company guy, but I'm just infantry. Okay, I know I've not seen any action, but I could have joined one of those scout groups, right?"

"No. They have us both in case one of us gets lost," Brookins explained over his shoulder at the trailing Hugh.

"Gets lost? Where? Here? But we're only talking about going from one end of town to the other. How are we going to get lost?"

Brookins paused to catch his breath, leaning against the wall of a pharmacy on a corner of the Grand Rue leading to the Hotel Claravallis. The sting of the cold early morning air felt good against his face. He was already sweating from the trot through town. Hugh stood next to Brookins leaning against the same wall.

"It's in case one of us is *lost*," Brookins repeated, this time looking Hugh in the eye.

"Oh, you mean . . . ," Hugh realized, war logistics and tactics understood.

"That's why they send us in pairs. The message still has to get through no matter what," Brookins stated. Taking a deep breath, he peered around the corner. More buildings burned, and thick billows of black, acrid smoke hung in the misty, frigid air. "Let's go," he said and the two hurried up the street to HQ.

They finally arrived at the Hotel Claravallis to find headquarters for the 110th Regiment in turmoil. Although Army Intelligence had warned frontline units that the Germans may be preparing to strike in small numbers, no one had expected an attack of this magnitude. The Americans were taken by surprise and were now being forced to devise a plan on the spur of the moment to stop this German advance, whatever it was and in whatever strength. Brookins and Harrington reported to the message center as instructed but were immediately sent back out to help evacuate civilians from Clervaux.

"Get down to the Hotel Koener," a lieutenant from the message center commanded, while pointing out the hotel on a wall map. "There's a transport truck there waiting. Get out as many people out as you can, and then report back."

After a brief sprint through town, Brookins and Harrington arrived at a small square across from the hotel. They immediately began herding people from across the square and then lifting them into the back of the waiting truck. Brookins had just helped get a woman and her young daughter into the truck when the woman began frantically yelling and pointing. Brookins didn't understand but looked to where she was motioning to see a little boy standing on his own across the square. Putting it all together, Brookins trotted over to the boy who looked to be about four years old.

"*Boom . . . boom*," said the boy mimicking distant mortar rounds as Brookins scooped him up and carried him over to the truck. They'd gone only a few yards when the square was ripped by a burst of gunfire. Bullets sizzled the air, striking building facades beyond. Brookins instinctively stopped in his tracks and hunched down while holding the boy.

"*Boom . . . boom,*" repeated the boy.

Brookins slowly turned to see a German soldier standing at the opposite end of the square no more than forty yards away, the muzzle of his still-smoking sub-machine gun pointed at him and the boy. Brookins quickly eyed the truck. Everyone heard the shots, saw the German, and took cover except the boy's frantic mother calling out from the back of the truck. Sizing up the distance between himself and the truck, Brookins knew he'd never make it. He also knew that any attempt to get to his M-1 carbine slung over his shoulder was pointless. Precious seconds hammered away. Brookins had seen more than his share of fighting and dying to know, for him, it was over. He tried to swallow, but his mouth was suddenly dry. He felt his chest tighten. He held his breath. He knew there was no way the German would miss again, not at this close range. A strangely soothing warmth washed over him with the world around now silent, stopped. Brookins accepted, in few seconds he would be dead. At least let it be quick and painless, no slow agonizing wounds. He closed his eyes while turning slightly, putting his back squarely between the gray-coated German soldier and the little boy, a last selfless gesture. The boy would make it no matter what.

It hit him in an instant, from the silence, from out of nowhere, like sniper's bullet the thought: *at this close range.* How did he miss *at this close range?* He couldn't have missed. No, he didn't miss, Brookins reasoned, that short burst went exactly where the German soldier had aimed; somewhere over their heads. To Brookins, everything became clear. He slowly straightened, all the while keeping his eye on the German standing at the ready, weapon pointed. Suddenly, deliberately, the German slowly pulled his gaze from Brookins and the boy and instead surveyed billows of smoke pouring from the third-story window of a mortar-damaged building just to his right. Brookins knew he was being given a chance. He hurried to the truck, heaved the boy up to his mother's arms and turned back in time to see the back of the enemy soldier disappearing up the street.

"Holy . . ."

"Time to go," Brookins declared, interrupting a clearly stunned Hugh Harrington. "Go!" Brookins yelled and waved to the truck driver.

The engine revved, belching gray smoke from the exhaust pipe. The truck juddered forward only a few feet when the windshield exploded in a hail of bullets, from where, no one was certain. Glass shards sliced into the driver's forehead at his hairline above the right eye, and a moment later blood poured from the deep gash. He looked over at the other soldier in the cab now slumped against the passenger door; holes in his face and neck oozing dark red, turning his uniform glossy black. Between gearshifts, the driver dabbed at the wound in his forehead with his coat sleeve, and with his one clear eye, he negotiated the streets of Clervaux. Brookins and Harrington watched the truck roll out of sight before they again dashed through the square, this time on their way back to HQ.

Despite the encounter with the German soldier, the incident with the truck at the far end of town, and mortar rounds that appeared to be falling randomly, Brookins and Harrington saw no signs of German activity in the center of Clervaux as they cautiously hurried back to the command post at the Hotel Claravallis.

"Halt!" yelled the GI on guard duty outside HQ, his rifle pointed at Brookins and Harrington, both stopping in their tracks. "Apple!" the guard called out.

"What?" a confused Brookins responded.

"Apple!" the guard challenged sternly, his finger wrapped around the trigger of his M-1 Garand rifle.

"Hang on, hang on! We don't know the response," Brookins stressed, his and Hugh's arms raised. "No one told us!"

"Identify yourselves!"

"We're with the 28th. He's Harrington from the 112th here on R&R and I'm Brookins . . . signal company. I'm here on TD to show movies to the guys."

The guard held his stare, sizing up the two soldiers while mulling over the information he'd just been given, his mind working.

"What movies?" the guard challenged anxiously.

"*Going My Way*."

"Who's the star?"

"Bing Crosby," Brookins sighed heavily with a roll of the eyes.

The guard looked over the two runners as he processed. After a few moments, he lowered his rifle. "All right," he said, easing the tension in his back and shoulders. "C'mon. And so you know for next time, the response is *brandy*."

"Got it, thanks," Brookins said as he and Hugh hustled past the GI guard and into the Claravallis. For the next few hours, Brookins and Harrington carried messages about German troop strength and movement as well as American defenses, countermeasures, and casualties back and forth between HQ and the few squad leaders and forward positions that could be found. It was late afternoon when Brookins and Harrington, taking a break in the lobby of the Claravallis and awaiting further orders, saw Colonel Hurley Fuller, the gruff, no-nonsense, World War I veteran step into the room.

Fuller, who had been given command of the 110th in late November, had just gotten off the phone with General Cota in Wiltz. All morning, Fuller's frontline units heroically beat back the initial German assault, but the day waning, the outnumbered and outgunned Americans were losing ground. Fuller had requested more troops being held in reserve, but the request was denied, citing the need to keep the troops in reserve in case this was some sort of diversionary assault.

"We've been ordered to hold, and I quote, 'at all costs,'" he barked tersely to his staff freezing in place at the news. "Get the word out. I don't care who it is. Tell anyone who can fight to grab whatever weapons and ammo they can find and take up positions throughout town. We're going to stop these Krauts right here. If all else fails, the castle, that's our Alamo. All right. Let's move!" With that, the room erupted with action. Colonel Fuller then spotted Brookins and Harrington. "You two," he pointed, "Get down to the Hotel Central and find Lieutenant Thompson. Tell him to get everybody out of there and rally whoever is left at the castle," Fuller ordered.

"Yes, sir," they said in unison and then dashed out of the hotel.

Brookins and Harrington hurried through the streets, the echo of battle encroaching on the valley town. Along with explosions near and far was ever-increasing small-arms fire and the portentous sound of squeaking and grinding from the mist-shrouded ridgeline road above. All around, buildings continued burning, filling the air with thick plumes of choking smoke. Along the Grand Rue—the main route leading to the Central Hotel—they dodged smoldering rubble and piles of debris littering the street.

While weaving through middle of town, on their left they could see the Parc Hotel perched high on the eastern ravine overlooking the town. Through the now-thinning mist, Brookins and Harrington saw German soldiers pouring over the lip of the ridge behind the hotel and swarming the surrounding hillside, affording a clear line of sight into Clervaux. This forced Brookins and Harrington to crouch low and hug a stone retaining wall at the bottom of the ravine along a section of the road to avoid becoming targets. The two runners moved quickly but cautiously, checking around corners and scanning the streets to be sure they wouldn't be seen. Rounding a corner near the end of the Grand Rue, they passed in front of the Hotel Bertemes, a short way down and across the street from the Central Hotel. It was then that Brookins suddenly realized that unlike the previous trips to this end of town, they hadn't seen any other GIs along the way. The street was unnervingly empty. They carefully approached Central Hotel and entered the deserted lobby. Hugh called out for others but there was no answer.

"Where is everyone?"

"Beats me," Brookins replied, his grip on his M-1 a little tighter. "Looks like they already got the word. C'mon, let's get out of here."

Harrington turned for the door, but Brookins grabbed him from behind. "Hang on," Brookins instructed as he shouldered past Hugh. "It's too quiet. Let's be sure the coast is clear." Brookins carefully slid himself into the left side of the doorway. He peered down the street to the right of the hotel. Seeing nothing, he moved to the other side of the doorframe and looked up the street to the left, from where they came. "Looks okay," he said, and the two slowly exited the hotel.

They trotted up the street, again past the Hotel Bertemes to the corner. After a quick check they proceeded back up the Grand Rue; a bit more urgency in their pace. Again they approached the stone retaining wall, stooping low when they spotted the bodies of three GIs lying at the base of the wall. As they approached, one of the GIs raised his head, startling Brookins.

"You guys hit?" Brookins asked, taking a knee.

"No, we're waiting for the Krauts," said the raised head. "We're going to surrender."

Again Brookins was stunned. This time however, he couldn't believe what he'd just heard. The thought of surrender repulsed him. He felt his stomach knot and his teeth clench.

"They're gonna get us. Look at 'em. They're gonna get us!" the second soldier blurted out hysterically. Brookins recognized him as a staff sergeant from the 112th.

"C'mon. What are you guys talking about? You're gonna surrender? How do you know they won't just shoot you right here? Look, come with us. We're heading up to HQ. They're going to rally everyone at the castle," Brookins implored.

"Look," said the third GI, another from Brookins' unit, "you can stay and fight 'em if you want, but look around. We ain't stopping 'em. And ya hear that? Those ain't Shermans up on that road, they're Panzers. The Krauts have this place surrounded."

"The only way we're getting out of this with our hides is if we give up. We ain't armed, and we're not puttin' up a fight. They can't shoot unarmed surrendering soldiers. It's part of the Geneva Convention. We'll take our chances as POWs," the first GI chimed in, a slight quiver in his voice.

Brookins stared at the three GIs, his face awash in disbelief. He knew they were scared, and for them this was their way of surviving. Brookins was scared too, but the thought of surrendering to the Germans was something he wanted no part of it. He glanced over at Hugh crouching down and clearly looking to Brookins for guidance.

"You can stay with these guys if you want," he said brusquely to Hugh, his anger misplaced, "but I sure ain't surrendering to any Germans," he added disdainfully then shuffled past the prone soldiers.

"I go where you go," Hugh declared without a moment's hesitation. "They send us in pairs, remember?" Although he'd only been in Luxembourg a short time and this was his first taste of battle, he wasn't about to let it end with his arms up in surrender. Hugh looked down at the three soldiers, shook his head, and then turned and followed Brookins along the wall.

The pair weaved quickly through town, without speaking about the three GIs and instead their attention on their task of getting back to the Claravallis. They were one turn away from the Grand Rue and the final sprint back to HQ when they heard German voices and boots on cobblestones coming from just up the road. Quickly and quietly, they scrambled, looking for cover. A moment later, Hugh spied the half-opened door to a closed-up butcher shop, and the pair ducked inside. They hastily closed the door and then stood off to the sides of what was left of the windows, flattening themselves against the walls, waiting as the sound of voices and heavy footfalls neared.

It was then that Hugh noticed a gently fluttering curtain covering an archway at the back of the small anteroom. He motioned to Brookins and pointed at the flapping curtain revealing flashes of orange flame behind whorls of black smoke in the next room. The building had been hit by an artillery shell, and what was left of the back half of it was on fire. Seconds later, the wave of German soldiers came trotting down the street. Brookins and Harrington were trapped. They pressed tight to the wall and held their breaths as the soldiers passed directly in front of the butcher shop. Brookins slid his finger from the side of the M-1 to the trigger. In his mind, he imagined the Germans entering the shop to finding them with just the one weapon and a fifteen-round magazine between them. As the scene played out in his mind, he knew that he may get one or two of them, but quickly the Germans would overpower them, and they would surely be killed. He would never see his mother, father, or fiancée, Virginia, again.

Still, he never thought of surrender. His thoughts were broken moments later with the telling sound of German voices and boots fading into the distance. Brookins and Harrington waited several minutes to be sure all the soldiers had passed. The flapping curtain finally surrendered, and heavy smoke now poured through the archway. There was no choice. They had to go. Hugh slowly opened the door, applying what he'd learned from Brookins at the Central Hotel. He surveyed up and down the street and looked over the nearby buildings in case Germans had gone inside any of them. He saw nothing.

Cautiously, the two men slipped out of the butcher shop and made their way up the street, sliding along the buildings and storefronts for as much cover as could be had. A few hundred yards up from the butcher shop, they approached a crossroad. A left turn would put them onto the Grand Rue leading back to HQ.

They were only a few steps from the crossroad when a two-man German machine gun team rounded the corner. The Germans, one carrying an MG-42 machine gun and the other ribbons of ammunition and a tripod, were no more than twenty yards away and were as startled to see the American soldiers as Brookins and Harrington were to see them. The four men stood squared, overcome by surprise and frozen with fear, staring at each other as the seconds lumbered by. In another time and another place, they might have raised a glass together as friends instead of raising weapons as enemies, but in this awkward moment of frozen time, the men now faced each other as duty-bound soldiers on opposite sides of a war.

The Germans moved, reaching for their rifles, and Brookins moved equally as fast, pressing the butt of his M-1 to his shoulder and pulling the trigger. Hugh dropped down, curled into a ball, and tried to shield himself behind a heap of rubble while backing flat against a storefront. Brookins pulled the trigger again and again, yelling to scare away the fear of shooting and of being shot and stopping only when the ammo clip was empty. The echo of the shots hung in the thick air and seemed to resonate endlessly through empty streets. Beyond the front sight on Brookins' rifle, he could see the two German soldiers now slumped over their machine gun.

Brookins stood frozen, breathless, his heart and mind racing, emotions churning. It was the first time he'd killed. He'd taken these two lives in a matter of seconds. It was his duty. It was what he'd been trained to do and what he had to do. He knew that the Germans would have shot the two of them, and after all, they were on their way to set up a machine gun somewhere ready to unleash death to who knows how many GIs that happened across its path. Yet in this moment of eerie stillness, in a way he couldn't understand, he felt different. He was different.

"Are you okay?" Hugh called out uneasily while getting to his feet.

"Yeah, I'm good," Brookins answered from somewhere far off. "But I never . . ."

"Do you think they're dead?" asked Hugh eyeing the Germans, their gray uniforms blackening.

"I don't know. I guess so," Brookins said, recoiling back to the moment. He ejected the spent clip, grabbed another from the pouch on the rifle stock and slapped it in. He cycled the action, readying his weapon. Taking a deep breath, he blinked away the moisture stinging his eyes. "Let's get out of here," he said firmly. "If those other guys heard the shots, they may head back this way."

Brookins and Harrington stepped to the corner and scanned the cross street. All clear. As they trotted up the street, Brookins stole a look back to where they'd been to see if any Germans were coming up behind them. The street was deserted, but out of the corner of his eye, through wafting smoke, he saw one of the soldiers he'd just shot roll over onto his side and raise a hand. Brookins turned away, hoping and praying that maybe they were still alive. Another deep breath, and with Hugh following, he began the final run back to HQ.

The two arrived to find the Hotel Claravallis in chaos. Regardless of the orders from command, it was now clear that without reinforcements,

Clervaux would soon fall. The 110th HQ was preparing to fall back. Brookins and Harrington spotted Colonel Fuller standing next to a blazing fireplace, the pile of documents he cradled fueling the fire.

"There was no one left back there, sir," Brookins reported.

"Okay. Good," Fuller responded while feeding the flames. "Look, fellas, I know you want to get back to your unit, but I'm afraid there's nothing we can do to help. We're going to hold as long as we can. That means you guys are on your own. It's every man for himself now. Consider yourselves relieved here. If I were you, I'd get out of here. Right now the road to Bastogne looks like the best way out. Good luck, boys," the colonel said, ending the conversation.

Brookins and Harrington exchanged looks, tossed out a "yes, sir," and then bolted for the door. The situation in Clervaux was getting desperate, and if they had any chance of getting out, it would be now or never. They were exhausted, cold, and wet from running all day through freezing mist. When and if they reached the road to Bastogne, the pair would then face a fifteen-mile hike back to Wiltz with the threat of Germans all around.

They fled the Hotel Claravallis, this time turning left away from the center of town and toward the road to Bastogne. Gone was the cold mist that accompanied them most of the day, replaced now by a high, gray sky with slashes of sunlight piercing through. Behind them, the streets of Clervaux teemed with GIs and vehicles all scrambling to get to the castle or somewhere. The sound of gunfire echoed all around, and what had earlier appeared to be random mortar hits throughout Clervaux were now targeted. Additionally, shells from German Panzers along the ridge were now finding their marks. What the Americans didn't know was that German loyalists were huddled in the basement of the pharmacy in the center of town, helping direct the barrage.

Brookins and Harrington sprinted a few hundred yards up the road toward the train station and the depot serving as a makeshift aid station for GIs on leave. Upon arrival, Brookins spotted an ambulance parked outside the depot with litters of wounded ready to be evacuated.

"Hey!" Brookins called out to a soldier standing near the ambulance. "Are you guys getting ready to head out?"

"In a few minutes," replied the captain from the medical corps. "But we're heading back to Wiltz."

"Oh, sorry, sir." Brookins hadn't realized the solder was an officer until he'd turned toward them. "We were hoping we could get a lift. That's where we're heading."

"You guys with the 112th?"

"Yes, sir. We were up here on TD and R & R when all hell broke loose. They assigned us as runners for HQ, but Colonel Fuller just relieved us and told us we're on our own."

"Well, you're in luck. We've got some room in the back if you want to come with us. We'll be leaving in a few. You can wait inside and warm up if you want," the captain offered, pointing at the depot with a clipboard.

Brookins and Harrington stepped inside the depot and stood shocked by the sight of a German soldier sitting in the depot on his own, unguarded. The soldier looked to be about thirty years old, wearing a battle-worn gray overcoat that loosely covered an equally tattered uniform, his face covered in days-old stubble and dirt. A teacher prior to the war, the *Wehrmacht* soldier had been in the army since 1940 and had seen more than his share of killing and dying and had had enough. Two nights earlier, he quietly left his post, crossed enemy lines under the cloak of pitch-black skies, and surrendered to one of the forward outposts of the 110th. He was blindfolded and then taken to HQ for interrogation, where he told of an impending large-scale attack in this sector sometime before Christmas. That and other more specific information gleaned from his questioning was quickly sent up the chain of command, where, for reasons unknown, it was set aside and ignored. Had the Allies acted on the information offered by this soldier as well as similar information presented by Allied sympathizers telling of a massive German build-up, there's no telling how many thousands of soldier and civilian lives may have been spared.

At this moment, however, Corporal Brookins stood arrow straight, his body flushed with anger at the sight of this enemy soldier. For Brookins, everything he'd seen or experienced in the war: the mud, blood, screams, and horrors of the Huertgen; the friends he lost there and elsewhere along the way; the fighting that now raged all around Clervaux; the surrendering GIs on the Grand Rue; the close call with that platoon of Germans in town; and the two machine gunners he shot was sitting before him. Brookins had a full magazine in his M-1, and right now he wanted nothing more than to empty it into this raggedy German. He gripped his rifle so tightly the knuckles in his hands began to ache, and the tendons in his wrists began to cramp. He was angry, and his anger swelled the longer he stood staring at the German soldier.

"*Schweinehund!*" Brookins suddenly shouted, startling both the German and Harrington. He spun around and stormed out of the depot. Harrington stood in place. He stared at the German, the frightened enemy soldier staring back. A few anxious moments passed between them, and then suddenly Hugh Harrington spat on the floor in front of the German, wiped his chin on the sleeve of his jacket, and followed Brookins outside.

The two stood in silence outside the depot. Brookins shouldered his rifle, stuffed his hands into his jacket pockets and closed his eyes. He tilted his head back and breathed deeply, filling his lungs with the still-crisp December air, letting the day's first burst of warming sun baptize his face.

"All set, sir," a soldier announced to the captain. The soldier then climbed into the cab of the ambulance behind the steering wheel and fired the engine.

"You guys still want that ride?" the Captain called over to Brookins and Harrington.

"Yes, sir," Harrington answered for them.

"Okay then. Let's go. They only thing is, you have to leave that here," the captain said, nodding at Brookins rifle.

"Why?" asked the puzzled Brookins.

"Red Cross regulations. No weapons. It's an ambulance," the captain said, pointing at the faded red on white insignia on the truck. Brookins and Harrington were dumbfounded. They wanted and needed to get back to Wiltz and their division's HQ. They were tired, cold, hungry, scared, and still a long way from Wiltz. There was no telling when or if they would encounter another American vehicle, let alone one that was heading into town. And then there were the Germans to think about. What would they do if they ran into more Germans? They weren't wounded, and they would be without the only weapon they had. No doubt they would be forced to surrender or worse.

"What's it going to be, fellas?" the captain asked impatiently. "Do you want a ride into Wiltz or not?"

"Sure, we want a ride, but I don't think we should leave behind the only weapon we have," Brookins answered.

"Look, it's the rules, okay?" the captain stressed. "Guys, if it was up to me, I'd say no problem. But it ain't up to me. I've got to follow orders too, you know. No weapon or no ride. That's it."

Hugh looked at Brookins, wondering what they should do. Brookins had gotten them this far, and Hugh trusted him to decide what would be best. He was trusting Brookins with his life.

"Never mind. We'll pass. Thanks anyway," Brookins finally said.

"All right. Suit yourself," the captain said, getting into the cab. Seconds later, the ambulance slowly rolled forward, turned onto the road, and headed out of sight.

"You think we did the right thing?" asked Brookins.

"After what happened with those Germans in town? Yeah, we did the right thing. We'll get back eventually somehow."

"Well, no sense waiting around here," Brookins said glancing back at the depot. "I don't think the next train's due for a while," he tried to joke.

With that, the two soldiers began their hike along the Bastogne road back to Wiltz. At that moment, the duo had no way of knowing that the road they were on was a major German objective and the reason for the attack on Clervaux. Seizing the bridges in town that crossed the Clerve River would allow German armor access to this road; It was one of the only relatively straight, paved roads in the Ardennes—a road that ran through Luxembourg and into Belgium to the tangled-crossroad town of Bastogne.

Brookins and Harrington walked along the road for about a quarter of a mile without seeing anyone or hearing anything except the distant sound of artillery that continued striking Clervaux. The sunlight that had accompanied them was beginning to fade, taking the warming temperatures with it. Increasing darkness would soon become a factor. The last thing they wanted was to be stuck in the middle of the Ardennes hills, frozen, alone, exhausted, without food, with only one weapon and the threat of Germans everywhere. Although neither spoke about it, they knew their situation could turn desperate.

They approached a fork in the road, with the road to Bastogne continuing to the left while the road to St. Vith on the right. Suddenly from the left came the sound of a roaring engine, and the pair looked up to see an American M-8 light armor car barreling down the road at top speed on its way to Clervaux. Brookins and Harrington watched the "Greyhound," as it was known, speed past them, motor down the road, and vanish from sight into the smoldering town. They turned back to continue their trek, but after only a few steps they heard the throaty moan of another engine, this time coming from up the road to the right. The dull diesel rumbling reverberated through the countryside. Then a white-starred two-and-a-half-ton American army truck vehicle rounded a long, sweeping bend in the road and downshifted as it approached the crossroads. It slowed to a near stop in anticipation of the sharp turn onto the road to Bastogne when Brookins stepped in front waving his arms.

"Where are you guys heading?" Brookins asked up to the driver. "Wiltz," came the reply from the driver leaning out of the window of the cab. "Why? What's up?"

"We're trying to get back there. We sure could use a ride."

"No problem. Hop on in," the driver said thumbing toward the back of the truck.

"Have you seen any Germans?" Hugh asked.

"Germans?" The driver seemed surprised by the question.

"Yeah, Germans," Brookins repeated. "They're on the move."

"On the move?" repeated the soldier, surprised.

"We just came from Clervaux. We got out of there in the nick of time. The last we saw, they had the town pretty much surrounded, and they were pushing through all our lines."

"Are you sure? We haven't heard anything about it."

"Yeah, I'm sure. Take a look. All that smoke is from the shelling. Like I said, we barely made it out. We really just need to get to back to Wiltz."

"In that case, you're in luck. We'll have you there in no time," the driver said, settling back into the cab and already grinding through the gears.

"Thanks!" Brookins said. Then he and Hugh hustled to the back of the truck. Hugh lifted up the canvas flap covering the back of the truck and hesitated from surprise.

"What the?" Brookins asked, looking into the truck bed. "I don't believe it. It's a laundry truck."

"Well, let's look at the bright side," Hugh said, wasting no time climbing in. "At least it's clean laundry."

As soon as they were both inside, Brookins rapped on the deck of the truck bed twice with the butt of his gun to signal the driver. The two soldiers nestled themselves amongst the heaps of laundry bags as the truck lumbered down the road. Brookins fished inside his jacket and pulled out a damp, crumpled pack of cigarettes. Disappointed, he balled-up the pack and tossed it aside.

"Just perfect."

"Hey!" Hugh exclaimed reaching into his jacket. "I forgot all about this," he said pulling out a metal flask as the truck bounced along. He unscrewed the cap and tried to see what was left in the flask, but it was too dark inside the truck. Instead he swished around the contents, and satisfied with his findings, leaned forward offering the flask to Brookins. "I found this stuff in town," Hugh explained as Brookins first sniffed at opening then downed a mouthful. He winced as the liquid burned the back of his throat. He could feel the warmth of alcohol tingle in his nose as it slid down his throat and into his stomach.

"What is that stuff?" Brookins gasped passing the flask back to Hugh, who took a swig, scrunched his face, and coughed.

"Apple!" Hugh challenged with a toothy grin.

"Huh?"

"Apple!" he challenged again, his smile wide.

"Brandy!" Brookins finally responded with a laugh as he collapsed back onto a pile of soft, clean clothes.

Left: Virginia Curry and her fiancé, Cpl. Richard Brookins, May 1943. *Photo: Richard Brookins*

Right: Harry Stutz, 1944.
Photo: Harry Stutz private collection

192267

Top left: 28th Infantry Division marches down the Champs Élysées, August 29, 2944. *Photo: National Archives*

Top right: Gen. George Marshall (center) at "Villa Adler" in Wiltz, October, 1944. *Photo: National Archives*

Bottom left: 28th Infantry Division MPs on patrol in Percy, France, 1944. The soldier nearest to the camera with his back turned is Sgt. Frank McClelland. *Photo: "28th Infantry Division in World War II"*

Bottom right: Gen. Dwight Eisenhower meeting soldiers from the 28th Infantry Division in Wiltz, November 1944. *Photo: National Archives*

Above (left to right): Maj. Gen. John W. Leonard, 9th Armor Division; Maj. Gen Troy Middleton, VIII Corps; Lt. Gen. Omar Bradley, 12th Army Group; Gen. Dwight Eisenhower, Supreme Allied Commander at the "Villa Adler" in Wiltz, November 1944. *Photo: National Archives*

Right: German POWs marching out of town after the fall of Aachen; December 1944. *Photos: National Archives*

Left: Photo of a German machine gun team during the Battle of the Bulge, December 1944. *Photo: National Archives*

Below: A bazooka team emerging from the woods outside of Wiltz after a night on watch at the beginning of the Battle of the Bulge, December 1944. *Photo: National Archives*

Opposite top: German soldiers captured in the Ardennes during the Battle of the Bulge, January 1945. *Photo: National Archives*

Opposite bottom: Soldiers from the 26th Infantry Division Cavalry Recon heading out of Wiltz, January 23, 1945. *Photo: National Archives*

Left: Rue De Tondeurs, Wiltz, looking toward the Grand Rue, 1945. *Photo: National Archives*

Below: View of the Grand Rue from the Rue de la Fountaine in Wiltz, 1945. (The tower at the entrance to Wiltz Castle is in the upper left portion of the photograph.) *Photo: National Archives*

Left: Richard Brookins in Germany, May 1945. *Photo: Richard Brookins*

Below left: Richard Brookins in Germany, May 1945. *Photo: Richard Brookins*

Below right: The bridge in lower Wiltz, 1945. *Photo: National Archives*

CHAPTER 11

1977

It was nearly eleven o'clock at night when a taxi dropped Frank McClelland off in front of his house. Frank had left Germany earlier that day and spent the better part of twelve hours in either an airplane or an airport. But now, finally, he was home.

Frank paid the driver and then picked up his one suitcase and marched up to the front door. He propped the storm door open with his foot as he pushed a key into the deadbolt, only to find that the lock wouldn't budge. Mumbling in frustration, he dropped his suitcase on the front stoop and gave the doorknob a sharp pull as he twisted the key. It now moved freely, reeling in the deadbolt. He opened the heavy door to the sound of crunching just inside the foyer. Frank rolled his eyes as his remembered that he hadn't made it to the post office to put his mail on hold before leaving. He picked up his suitcase and stepped in across the pile of mail and felt along the wall for the light switch. The house had an empty, stale smell from being closed up for ten summer days. Frank dropped his suitcase on top of the mail pile and walked across the living room. Having no air conditioner, he opened a couple of windows on the side of the house, letting the air of the summer night cool and revive the stale rooms. Back in the foyer, he picked up his suitcase and climbed the stairs to the bedroom. *The mail would still be there in the morning,* he thought. Now all he wanted to do was to get a solid night's sleep in his own bed.

Inside the bedroom, Frank opened his suitcase and hastily unpacked, throwing nearly all the clothing into the hamper except for a few clean pairs of socks and underwear. He carried his shaving kit into the bathroom and put the contents in their usual places.

Returning to the bedroom, Frank set the suitcase aside and opened one of the windows. He closed his eyes and breathed in the fresh night air scented with honeysuckle that grew wild along the fence in his yard. He flopped onto the bed. Despite the house being closed up, the fresh sheets he'd put on the day he left for Europe seemed cool and comforting. He sighed, closed his eyes, and in a few minutes was fast asleep.

The next morning, Frank woke up and realized he had fallen asleep in his clothes. He hadn't planned on doing that, but the traveling and jet lag had gotten the better of him. He went downstairs to the kitchen and started a pot of coffee before jumping into the shower and putting on some clean clothes. After dressing, he returned to the kitchen, this time stopping at the foyer to pick up the mail piled on the floor. As he sat at the kitchen table with his coffee, he sorted through the mail, separating out the bills and other important letters. Everything else went into the nearby trash can unopened. Tomorrow was Tuesday, and he'd be going back to his job as a route foreman with the Port Authority Transit; but for today, the last day of his vacation, there was laundry and shopping to do, as well as paying some of the bills he'd just opened. He also wanted to get his suitcase back into the attic before the summer sun began beating down on the slate roof and the attic became too hot. The last place Frank wanted to be on a hot summer day was in the attic.

He went upstairs and grabbed the suitcase from under the window where he'd left it. Carrying the bag to the closet, he pulled a dangling string to turn on the light and pushed aside the clothes at one end of the closet. Behind the clothing lay a small landing, and above it, framed into the ceiling, was a piece of painted plywood.

Frank positioned himself on the landing to get some leverage and pushed at the center of the plywood, moving the board upward until it cleared the attic floorboards. He then slid the piece of plywood to the right along the attic floor. It was midmorning, and already Frank could feel hot, stifling air collecting in the recess above him. He reached up and pulled at the string to turn on the attic light. He then hopped down from the landing and grabbed the suitcase.

Hoisting the bag up on to the landing, he opened it one more time to make sure he'd taken everything out before storing it. He felt around in the inner pockets to make sure they were empty too. As he did, he came across a folded piece of notepaper. He unfolded the paper and suddenly remembered that it had been given to him by one of the men he'd met in Wiltz. He opened it and read the name "Jeanly Schweig" along with an address and a telephone number.

Frank stuffed the paper into his shirt pocket and closed the suitcase before shoving it through the opening in the ceiling. It landed with a thud on the attic floor. Frank switched off the lights and closed everything up again before heading back down to the kitchen table. There at the table, he pulled the crumpled paper from his pocket and smoothed it out. On the bottom half of the paper under Schweig's name and address were the words, "Richard Brookins, Rochester."

Frank sat back in his chair, contemplating what to do. He had promised the men in Luxembourg that he would try to find Brookins when he returned home, and now that he was, he still didn't know how to go about it armed with nothing more than a name and a town from a thirty-year-old photo caption. Just outside the kitchen window, determined bees worked the honeysuckle flowers as Frank stared, pondering.

He took another sip of coffee, brewed strong that morning just the way he liked it. He placed the mug down on the envelope of the telephone bill he'd just opened. Frank's mind raced. He reached into a cupboard drawer just under the phone and retrieved an old address book stuffed thick with so many scraps of paper that it closed only with the aid of a thick rubber band. He opened the book and began sorting through the yellowed pieces of paper until he found the one he wanted. He grabbed for the phone on the kitchen wall and began dialing. The phone rang several times before there was a click and a voice on the other end.

"Bell of Pennsylvania. How may I direct your call?"

"Extension 219, please," Frank said. A series of clicks peppered the line, then ringing again.

"David Kelly," a voice declared.

"Dave, it's Frank McClelland. How have you been?" Frank asked his old National Guard buddy.

"Frank! How are ya?" Dave said with surprise.

"Fine, fine. How are you doing?"

"Great, thanks. I haven't heard from you in—how long has it been?"

"Yeah, I know. It's been awhile. I think the last time was at the reunion, remember?"

"Yes, I do remember. It's good to hear from you."

"Listen, the reason I'm calling—you obviously still work for the phone company, right?"

"Obviously. Almost twenty years now, why? You looking for a job?" Kelly kidded.

"Sure, I'd like something that pays a hundred grand a year, but I only want to work three days a week and only from eleven to one," Frank laughed. "Actually the real story is, well it's kind of hard to explain, but I was wondering if you could help me find a guy."

"Find a guy? You mean a number? Have you tried information?"

"Well, no I haven't," Frank began to explain. "You see I just came back from Europe . . ."

"No kidding!" Kelly interjected with genuine surprise.

"Yeah, I just got back yesterday. It's not my first time back there, but this time I visited a bunch of places. Kind of retracing my steps from during the war. I always said I was going to do it someday, and with Grace gone and the kids on their own, well I figured, why not?"

"No kidding. How was it?"

"It was good. I went to Germany, France, Belgium, and Luxembourg. I rented a car and just drove all over."

"Gee, Frank. That sounds great."

"Oh, it was. The weather was good, and this time I got to face down some demons."

A brief, strained silence passed over the phone. Kelly knew all too well that his old friend had long been troubled by his war experiences, especially his time as a POW. Frank rarely slept well due to persistent nightmares; he had difficulty in large social gatherings and was often depressed—a condition for which he was under a doctor's care. Frank always believed the problems had when he came home were the direct result of his capture and the crushing weight of responsibility he shouldered for the deaths of his friends that one December day. Frank had difficulty speaking to anyone about his problems, but Dave Kelly, his long-time friend and fellow National Guard veteran, was one of the people he would talk to on occasion. In fact, it was David who eventually convinced Frank to talk to someone at the VA hospital. Hearing him admit that he had finally met at least some of his ghosts head-on was, in Kelly's mind at least, an enormous step for Frank.

"Anyway, here's the thing," Frank continued, breaking the awkward silence, "while I was in Luxembourg, I ran into these locals over there and, well, to make a long story short, I told them I'd help find this guy that served over there during the war. The problem is, all I've got is a name and the town where he lived thirty years ago."

"Wait. I don't get it. You need to find someone from a town over in Europe?" a confused Kelly asked.

"No, no. The guy they're looking for is an American. He was a GI over there during the war, like us. We were all in the 28th, though I didn't know the guy. Anyway, some of the people of this one town asked me if I would help them try to find him. They figured that since we were in the same division that maybe I'd have better luck tracking him down than they did," Frank explained.

"Are you kidding?"

"No! They really want to find this guy. And honestly, I don't even know if he made it out of the war. And even if he did, I don't know if he's in the same town. So I didn't think I could just call information, you know? Then I remembered that you worked for the phone company, and I thought maybe you'd be able to feed the name into a computer or something."

"I'd like to help you out, Frank, but they don't let us use phone company records for personal use. They've got some serious rules against that sort of thing," Kelly explained.

"Oh, I didn't realize. Well, look, I don't want to get you in any trouble or anything. Like I said, I was just trying to help out these guys in Luxembourg. They're the ones who really wanted to find this guy because of what he did for them during the war, I guess."

"So what's the story with this guy? Is he Audie Murphy or something? What'd he do? Win the war?"

"Well, I don't really know. They have some sort of project or something they want to talk to him about."

"Listen, Frank, I tell you what. I can't do anything right now. I'm in the middle of something, but why don't you give me the guy's name and address or whatever you have, and I'll see what I can do. I can't promise you anything. Like I said, I really shouldn't be doing this sort of thing."

"Thanks, Dave. Whatever you can do would be great, and if ya can't do anything, that's okay too. I promised I'd try, so that's what I'm doing," Frank said. "Anyway the guy's name is Richard Brookins, and he came from Rochester, New York."

"*Brookins*, you said?"

"Yes, that's right. Richard Brookins. B-R-O . . ."

"O-K-I-N-S," Kelly finished. "Richard Brookins? And he was in the 28th? A signal company guy, right?"

"Yeah, I guess," McClelland confirmed, with a note of suspicion.

"And he was with the signal company, *correct?*" Kelly pressed.

"What?" Frank asked, his voice adrift. "Wait . . . how did you know . . . ?"

"Frank! I know this guy!" Kelly announced excitedly.

"You do?"

"You bet I do. Well, if it's the same guy, I know him. It's gotta be him. How many guys have the same name and live in Rochester? Sure, it's the same guy. He was one of my guys in basic. I taught him how to use the SIGABA equipment. I remember because he was pretty sharp, caught on quickly.

"And . . . ," Kelly paused, collating his thoughts and memories, "he's one of the guys that shut down all coded communications all over the world for almost a month. I'm serious," he said with a chuckle. "It happened in Colmar, France in '45. Early February, I'm pretty sure. They were setting up divisional headquarters there and had the SIGABA on a truck parked right outside where they were billeted. They just got into town, and there was no motor pool set up at the time, so they were told to just park the truck on the street near where they were staying. Now, someone was supposed to put a guard on that truck. It was SOP what with the SIGABA being highly classified, but they forgot. Next morning, your guy Brookins comes down with another fella, and guess what? The truck is gone. *Pfft.* Just gone. No others, just that one. So they went looking for it, thinking maybe the motor pool got set up overnight and someone moved it there, but nope. Vanished. So they alerted the CO, and like wildfire, it went up the chain of command all the way to Ike, who made finding the truck and, more important, the SIGABA a top priority. Everyone was afraid that maybe the Germans had gotten ahold of the machine, so they had to take precautions. All coded messages stopped. Shut down completely. Think about it. Even FDR in the White House couldn't talk to Churchill in England because it all went through this coding machine. Okay, so Brookins wasn't actually the guy that shut it all down. Just the poor guy to discover that the truck was gone. But still, it was a pretty big deal at the time."

"Did they ever find the thing?"

"Oh, sure. Not until about a month later when they found the truck abandoned in a field with no SIGABA. It was still missing. They ended up finding it later that afternoon in a river. I guess whoever stole the truck couldn't figure out how to open the safe to get to whatever was inside, so they just dumped it. Anyway, it all started with your guy Brookins.

"Hey . . . ," Dave's voice trailed off in thought for moment, "Frank, you're not going to believe this, but now that you've got me thinking, I'm pretty sure Brookins even works for the phone company!"

"I don't believe it!"

"Now, I haven't spoken to him in a while. We tried to keep in touch when we got back after the war, but you know how it is. We try to find the time to talk every now and again. Listen, tell ya what I'll do. Let me look up his number, and I'll pass it along. Then I'll get ahold of him and let him know you want to speak to him. How's that sound?"

"That sounds great. You know, Dave, when you stop to think about it, what are the odds? I mean, here I am in Wiltz, these guys ask me to help locate a soldier from thirty years ago, I agree, get home, call you for help, and you actually know the guy! And he's alive and well! That's pretty remarkable, don't ya think?"

"Miraculous, I'd say! What a coincidence. Listen, give me your number again too. I know I have it at home but not here at the office. As I said, I'll give Dick a call and get back to you, okay?"

"Sounds great, Dave," Frank said and then recited his phone number. "Thanks a bunch. Beers on me next time, okay?"

"I'm going to hold you to that!" Kelly joked.

"You got it. Thanks again, Dave," Frank said as he hung up the phone.

He sat for a moment, stunned by the unfolding of events and buoyed with excitement. Not only had he fulfilled his promise to help find Brookins, but he'd actually done it.

Frank put the yellowed scrap of paper that held David Kelly's name and phone number back in the address book and returned the book to the drawer. There were plenty of chores he needed to do before returning to work the following day. On a piece of scrap paper, he began jotting down a list of things he would need from the grocery store. He took a moment to clear the refrigerator of everything he thought had spoiled while he was away and checked the results against his list. He then went upstairs to grab the clothes hamper out of the bedroom. As Frank descended the stairs, he tried to organize the day in his mind, starting with the laundry.

After loading a pile of clothes into the washing machine, he would go to the grocery store and get what he needed. By that time, the clothes would be done and he could throw them into the dryer. Then he planned to go outside and mow the overgrown lawn.

Frank hauled the hamper down to the basement and dumped its contents onto the cellar floor. He opened the shutoff valves mounted on the basement wall and pulled the knob on the washing machine to turn on the water. As the tub began filling, he added the detergent and clothes. He always used warm water in the wash cycle and cold in the rinse cycle, that way, he thought, he wouldn't have to sort out the whites and the colors. He could just throw everything in together and wash it all at once. Frank closed the lid of the washing machine and pulled at the control knob just as the phone on the kitchen wall began ringing. He sprinted up the stairs to the kitchen and grabbed at the handset.

"Hello?" he barked into the phone with an obviously winded voice.

"Frank? Is that you?" the voice on the other end of the line asked.

"Yes, who's this?"

"It's Dave Kelly! Don't tell me you forgot already!" he needled.

"No, no. Of course not. I just ran up from the basement. I didn't recognize your voice," Frank explained.

"Listen, I didn't talk to Dick because he's still at work, but I left a message with his wife. Her name's Virginia. I told her to let him know that you'd be calling sometime soon. I hope that's okay."

"Okay? It's fantastic. Thanks, Dave I really appreciate this. Let me get a pen."

Kelly recited Brookins' phone number and address. To be sure he heard it correctly, Frank read both back to Kelly.

"Okay. Remember, you owe me beers for this one."

"Dave, you can count on it," Frank assured him cheerfully. "I'll buy you the whole keg! Thanks for the help. I really appreciate it."

"No problem. Maybe when we're having those beers, you can fill me in on what this is all about."

"Well as soon as I find out what's going on, you've got a deal. Thanks again. We'll see ya."

Frank sat down at the kitchen table and stared at the information he had just written down. He wondered what to do next, especially because hadn't thought this far ahead since he really hadn't believed he'd be able to find Richard Brookins, let alone get a phone number and an address.

He looked at the clock and wondered when he would make the call and, most important, what he would say. Frank began rehearsing his part of the conversation, how he'd introduce himself, and what he'd say to steer the conversation, trying to get the words and phrasing just right. After about twenty minutes he looked at the clock on the kitchen wall. He thought for a moment and then finally picked up the phone and dialed.

"Operator," a voice announced.

"Yes, I'd like to make a long-distance call . . . to Luxembourg."

CHAPTER 12

Dick Brookins was sitting comfortably on the sofa in his living room, watching the evening news, when the phone on the end table rang. He had arrived home from work, and his wife, Virginia, greeted him with the news that his old army buddy David Kelly had called earlier that day and left a message: that a former soldier from the 28th Infantry Division named Frank McClelland might be calling, wanting to speak with him about something that happened during the war. Throughout dinner that evening, Brookins was uncomfortably nervous, sporadically peppering Virginia with questions.

"And he didn't say why he wanted to speak to me?"

"No, Dick. David only said that this man had called looking for you and that he had given him our number."

"Well, I don't know what he wants to speak to me about. I've never even heard of this guy. Did David say what he did during the war? What unit he was in?"

"Dick, he only said this Frank person was looking to speak to you and that he too had been in the war."

On the fourth ring, Brookins finally picked up the handset. "Hello?" he called into handset with a hint of trepidation in his tone.

"Is this Richard Brookins?" quizzed the voice on the other end of the line.

"It is."

"Mr. Brookins, my name is McClelland, Frank McClelland. I hope I'm not calling at a bad time.

"No, it's fine. My wife told me David Kelly had given you our number."

"Yes, that's correct. I called David in hopes of finding you, because I knew he worked for the phone company and thought he could help me find you. Low and behold, it turns out he's a friend of yours and mine for that matter."

"Well, that's true. David and I have known each other since the war. He was my teacher back in basic."

"I know. He told me," Frank assured. "He was in the 28th too, as was I. I was a sergeant with the MPs."

"Is that so?" Brookins said, his curiosity overwhelming. "I was a corporal with the signal company message center."

"I know," Frank said, "and that's the reason I wanted to talk to you. Do you have a few minutes?"

With that Frank began relating the tales of his travels to Europe and in particular his most recent visit to Luxembourg. He started by telling Brookins about his wartime experiences, especially his time in Wiltz during "the Bulge" as the soldiers called it. He spoke about narrowly escaping Wiltz after the Germans ambushed the column of retreating soldiers; his harrowing journey through the woods outside Doncols; his capture by the Germans; his time in a POW camp and eventual liberation by advancing Russian troops. That was then followed by months of recovery in an army hospital, where he was treated for malnutrition, dysentery, dehydration, and bronchitis, all of which wreaked havoc on his body. Eventually the war ended, and he was shipped stateside and discharged. That's when he went back to work with the port authority.

After hearing Frank's accounting of the war, Brookins volunteered his own version beginning with "the Bulge" and his escape from Clervaux and then his return to Wiltz in a laundry truck. Upon arrival back at HQ, he was questioned by officers eager and desperate for information on the German attack. Three days later, on the morning of December 19, he was part of an advance detail tasked with establishing a divisional HQ in the town of Sibret on the southwestern outskirts of Bastogne. Driving through heavy snow and sleet with near-zero visibility, they arrived and immediately set about off-loading the top-secret SIGABA cryptography equipment. However, even through the heavy snow, they could see German soldiers in the distance advancing up the road. Under no circumstances was the SIGABA equipment to fall into enemy hands, so protocol dictated that the equipment be destroyed using a thermite block triggered with batteries. As luck would have it, the batteries failed, leaving them no choice but to put everything back on the trucks and fall back even further to the town of Neufchâteau on the French boarder, where they dug in, eventually stopping the German advance.

There was an awkward silence on the phone with both men lost in the memories.

"Actually, you mentioned Wiltz, and that's the reason I'm calling," Frank finally spoke. "You see, I just got back from there. I was sort of retracing my steps during the war, and well, I stopped in Wiltz. That's when I met these two guys, and it seems they've been trying to find you for a while."

"Wait, I don't understand. You met two guys over there in Wiltz who are trying to find me? Two GIs?"

"No, two men from the town—from Wiltz. Apparently, they've been looking for you for a while but haven't had much luck until I stumbled into town."

"I still don't understand," said Brookins with hint of frustration creeping into his tone. "There are a couple of guys from Wiltz who are looking for me? What for?"

"I really don't know. There's this one guy named Schweig, and he said he really wanted to find you. He even showed me your picture when you apparently dressed up as Saint Nicolas there during the war?"

Brookins sat straight up on the edge of the sofa, speechless against the enormous tidal wave of memories flooding his mind. In an instant, more than thirty years vanished, and Cpl. Richard Brookins was once again standing in courtyard of the Wiltz castle. He could feel the uneven cobblestones beneath his feet and the cool breeze blowing the priest's ropes he wore. He could hear the children singing and could see their eyes wide with excitement. He could smell the smoke from wood stove fires and hot chocolate.

"Are you still there?" asked Frank.

"Yes . . . I am," Brookins answered from Wiltz. "I mean, yes. Yes, I'm here. Wait, what's this all about?"

Frank realized the impact of what he'd just said and tried to explain away the shock. "Look, I know this comes out of nowhere, but when I was there, these two guys took me to this museum at the castle. It's tiny, but the whole thing is dedicated to everyone who fought in Wiltz, especially our division. And there on one of the walls is a picture of you dressed as Saint Nicolas, riding in a jeep."

Brookins remembered the photograph. It was the one that his mother had clipped from the *Rochester Democrat* newspaper; the same picture that was in an edition of the *Stars and Stripes* that had been stored away in a decades-old footlocker up in the attic.

"Wait, so this picture is in the museum there?"

"Yes. They have several, all from that day when I guess you played Saint Nicolas for the kids. Anyway, that's why I'm calling. One of the guys I met—as I said, his name is Schweig, Jeanly Schweig—he's been trying to locate you for a while. So when I arrived in town, they asked me if I could help out."

"And you don't know why they've been looking for me?" Brookins quizzed.

"I'm sorry. I don't. All I know is that they've been looking for you but without any luck. Then I happened into town, and suddenly they're asking me all these questions and wanting to know if I can help track you down. Really, I'm sort of just the go-between here. I've passed along your information to this guy Schweig in Wiltz. I'm sure he's going to call or send a letter or something that explains all of this. As I said, I promised them I'd try to find you and, well, my work is done."

"Listen, I appreciate the call. Can I get your number in case I have any questions for you?"

Brookins jotted down Frank's information, and the two ended the conversation with the promise to talk again and maybe get together someday. After hanging up the phone, Brookins sat lost for a while before finally getting up and walking to the hallway. He pulled at a piece of rope hanging from a trap door in the ceiling, opening a set of folding stairs to the attic. He climbed up until he could reach the piece of string attached to the light and gave it a tug. Instantly, the bare bulb spilled its light onto the clutter of the attic.

Brookins looked over to the far wall and spotted a dusty green trunk that had been tucked away in the corner of both the attic and his mind for years. He climbed the rest of the stairs and, crouching below the rafters, made his way to the trunk. Inside were his old army clothes, and on top sat a piece of yellowed newspaper pressed between two pieces of clear plastic wrap. Brookins lifted the paper and tilted it toward the attic light. His eyes pored over the well-faded newspaper photo showing a young man in priest's robes riding in an army jeep. He remembered coming home after the war and his mother telling him about that picture, the one that was seen in newspapers all across the country. She told him about the hundreds of cards and letters she had received from mothers who had seen that picture in their local newspapers and whose sons were also fighting in the war. They told her how lucky she was to know her son was alive and well and bringing so much joy to the poor children in Wiltz.

Brookins closed the lid of the trunk and climbed back down from the attic, the yellowed newspaper article still clutched in his hand. He walked into the kitchen, where Virginia had just finished clearing up after dinner, having left Dick on his own to talk to Frank.

"I take it that was Frank McClelland on the phone. Is everything okay?" she asked noticing the yellowed newspaper in her husband's hand and the dumbfounded look across his face.

"Do you remember this . . . ?

CHAPTER 13

In the days following the phone call from Frank, Dick had been expecting some sort of communication from Luxembourg, but none came. Days turned into weeks, and Brookins had all but forgotten about their conversation until arriving home one hot August evening to find a letter on the kitchen table bearing Luxembourg postage, postmarked from Wiltz.

The handwritten, four-page letter from Jeanly Schweig was dated August 5 and began with, "Dear Saint Nicolas. . . ." By way of introduction, the fifty-year-old Schweig explained that he and his wife of twenty-one years, Anna-Louise, still lived in the same home, above what had been his father's butcher shop in Wiltz close to the Grand Rue. They had six children, and at one time he had taken over the family's butcher shop until health problems forced him to close the shop in 1963. He now worked twenty miles from Wiltz as a plant supervisor for the Goodyear Tire Co.

In 1944, Schweig was only sixteen years old and had witnessed many friends and relatives a few years older than he go into hiding or be forced to fight in the German army. He remembered the American liberators who saved Luxembourg from the hated Nazis, and he vividly remembered the Saint Nicolas party in Wiltz. Once the war ended, Schweig vowed to always remember the American soldiers who fought and died to liberate Luxembourg, especially Wiltz. He had played a guiding role in the creation of monuments to Generals Eisenhower and Patton, as well as a monument outside Wiltz Castle dedicated to the soldiers of the

28th Infantry Division. Schweig went on to say that the soldiers from the signal company message center, especially Brookins, have never been forgotten in Wiltz. The letter read in part:

> "Be assured that you have never been forgotten here in Wiltz, since years I have the idea and was making research to locate you, but I never arrived to get your address, until I was spoken about you with and to Frank McClelland. . . . And now I come to explain to you my newest project, which I have the intention to realize next.
>
> The 6th of Dec. 1944, it happened here in Wiltz, that the 28th signal corps organized a Saint Nicolas Party for the kids of Wiltz, and the distribution of candies, goodies also, was done by their own means. That's a fact, and had never been forgotten. During the Bulge, which started 2 weeks later on 15th. Wiltz was nearly completely destroyed, and we needed a certain time to rebuild it. Then in 1947, we remembered the St. Nicolas party offered to Wiltz's kids 3 years earlier, and decided to make this traditional."

Brookins could hardly believe what he was reading. For him, that one December day in 1944 had been just that—one day. The war went on, and once he and the other soldiers were forced to leave Wiltz, they never went back. Now to see in writing what that one small party meant all these years later was overwhelming. He took off his glasses and dabbed at his eyes and then continued reading:

> "And now I am coming to the aim of this letter. As this year we are going to celebrate the 30th anniversary of the foundation of the St. Nicolas festival, we want to do something special. As my research concerning yourself, have been now successful, and I have located you after all, I have the idea, as the members of the 28th signal corps were the authors of the Wiltz St. Nicolas festival, I will try to fill you once again with enthusiasm to take over the part of playing St. Nicolas on this 30th anniversary."
>
> "Now it depends on you to make this my plans coming true. The whole Wiltz is waiting for you, please, if any how possible don't disappoint us."

Brookins sat back in his chair and thought. He leafed through the pages of the letter several times to be sure he had read and understood everything correctly. He looked up at Virginia who had sat down across from Dick, unnoticed.

"I think we need to plan a vacation," he said.

Richard Brookins' return to Wiltz began at the small airport in Rochester, New York. Though he usually had no trouble sleeping on airplanes, especially on long flights, Brookins now found it difficult to do anything but gaze out the window and think about Wiltz. With eleven hours of planes and airports ahead of him, he had plenty of time.

It had been four children, one grandchild, four promotions, two houses, four mortgages, eight cars, two dogs, and a lifetime since he had last seen or even thought of the sleepy little town nestled in the Luxembourg countryside. In fact, the last time he had been in Wiltz was the day the Germans attacked the town at the beginning of the Battle of the Bulge.

Brookins stared out at the wispy clouds floating far beyond the jet's wingtip. In the attic of his mind, he opened the dusty footlocker where he'd stored away his memories of Wiltz and the war. He thought about the Christmas party and the happy faces of the children. He thought about the GIs who had given from their hearts and made the day special for the children. He also recalled the scramble to get out of Clervaux ahead of the attacking Germans as he and Hugh Harrington had tried to get back to Wiltz. He wondered about the German soldiers he had to shoot—still hoping in his heart that they had made it. He thought about the ambulance that had offered to take him and Hugh to Wiltz, but only if they left their only weapon behind, and the laundry truck that finally got them back to town on a pile of clean clothes. He thought about Hugh.

As the muffled rumbling of the jet engines droned on, Brookins continued to summon long-forgotten memories of the turmoil he and Harrington encountered upon their return to Wiltz. The Germans were coming fast, and despite the courageous efforts of the forward companies, it was obvious that the 28th Division was spread too thin to stop the German assault. After three days of fighting in the surrounding hills, the division had no choice but to abandon its headquarters and fall back. For Richard Brookins and the other soldiers in the Keystone Division, December 19, 1944, had been a sad and painful day.

When Brookins and his family stepped off the plane in Luxembourg City, they were greeted by Jeanly Schweig and three other members of the Oeuvre Saint Nicolas. Brookins had only spoken to Jeanly a few times, and he didn't know any of the other men, yet he was welcomed as if they had known him all their lives and as if he were some distant cousin or uncle finally returning home after being away for years. In a way, these men *had* known Brookins all their lives, if only from the museum pictures and the story that had been passed down over the years.

The members of the Oeuvre Saint Nicolas drove the Brookins family to Wiltz. Along the way, Brookins stared out at the rolling hills of the Ardennes and tried to catch a glimpse of something he might recognize. Aside from the countless pine trees and hardwoods that stretched skyward, Brookins saw nothing except the occasional roadside monument or plaque dedicated to the soldiers who fought and died on nearby battlefields. Such tributes now dotted the countryside, honoring those who gave their lives to secure freedom for the people of Luxembourg.

Brookins and his family were taken to the Hotel Du Commerce, where they stayed for the week and where a reception and dinner were planned in Brookins' honor the night before the big celebration.

Throughout the week, Brookins spent his days getting reacquainted with the town he'd know for only a few weeks in 1944. Everywhere he went, people from the town would stop to meet him and shake his hand. Many of those who greeted him spoke some English; others spoke only German, French, or Lëtzebuergesch; but regardless of the language, they all knew how to say "American Saint Nicolas."

On the day of the reception, Brookins made it a point to visit several places in and around Wiltz. His first stop took him to Wiltz Castle and the museum. He took his time looking at the displays that portrayed major events of the war years. There were photos and artifacts from major battles, as well as displays honoring the people of Wiltz who organized the general strike. The museum also included photographs detailing the events of December 5, 1944, when the American Saint Nicolas arrived in Wiltz.

Brookins spent a good amount of time reading the captions and staring at the pictures. Of course he remembered every detail of what had happened that day, but he could not remember anyone taking pictures. The evidence was neatly arranged on the wall in black and white photographs, but no matter how he tried to peer through the mist of time, he could not recall seeing anyone with a camera.

As the photos sparked more memories, he chuckled over how nervous he had been riding in the jeep and meeting the children. He recalled being afraid that if he made a mistake, the people would never forgive him. As he studied the display, he remembered wearing the bishop's miter and how tight it had been. He remembered all these details, but he just could not remember seeing a camera.

After his stop at the castle, Brookins and Frank McClelland (McClelland had arrived a day after Brookins) visited a large stone memorial dedicated to the soldiers of the 28th Infantry. As relatives, townspeople, local military personnel, and members of the press looked on, Brookins and McClelland placed a large wreath at the base of the memorial. The wreath was a solid circle three feet in diameter and made entirely of roses: white on the outside with red roses arranged in the shape of the 28th Division's keystone shoulder patch in the center. After placing the wreath, Brookins and McClelland took a few steps back and paused to remember their fellow soldiers, many of whom never made it out of Wiltz.

Brookins' final stop before the reception was the American Military Cemetery in Hamm, just outside of Luxembourg City. More than five thousand American soldiers were buried there in razor-straight rows that radiated out from a central monument, with a white stone cross or Star of David marking each neatly manicured grave. Many of the men were victims of the fighting during the Battle of the Bulge. At one end of the massive field lay the grave of General George S. Patton, whose US Third Army had been headquartered in Luxembourg City and who had died shortly after the war.

Brookins walked among the graves, reading the names of the soldiers, until he came across one more memory—the grave of Edgar Stine. Eddie was another of Brookins' friends who stayed behind in Wiltz—one who never made it out. Tears welled up in Brookins' eyes as he read Eddie's name chiseled into the stone cross.

"We won, Eddie. We won," Brookins said softly. He bent down to place some flowers on Eddie's grave. He wiped the tears from his eyes, and after a few minutes of remembering his good friend, turned and walked away.

By the time Brookins arrived back at the hotel, he had put away the sorrow and pain of the day's visits, choosing instead to think about the reception that night and the Saint Nicolas ceremonies the next day.

The dining hall of the Hotel Du Commerce was filled to capacity that evening with dignitaries, local clergy and schoolteachers, representatives from the US Ambassador's office, and some of the townspeople who were there the first time Brookins played Saint Nicolas. There was also a camera crew on hand to film the entire event for NBC news.

The room erupted with cheers and applause as Brookins and his wife and family stepped into the room. A bit unnerved by the attention, Brookins smiled awkwardly and waved to the crowd. As he glanced around the room, his attention was drawn to a corner where he spotted a small, bald man with a round face, wide smile, and bright eyes. Brookins hurried over to embrace him.

"You son-of-a-gun," Brookins said, his voice cracking with emotion as he wrapped his arms around the man. "Did you know about all this?"

"Sure I knew," beamed Harry Stutz. "Do you remember the little girl Martha from back in '44? Well, she's all grown up now and has stayed in touch with me through the years. When she told me about this thirtieth anniversary celebration and said you were coming back, well, I wouldn't have missed this for anything."

"I really can't believe all this. People have been coming up to me since I got here; shaking my hand, hugging me, and showing me pictures from the war. It's amazing. I had no idea this was such a big thing."

"I guess they never forgot about us, eh?"

"You can say that again. You know, Harry, this is all because of you, really."

"Well, we were all involved, remember?"

"Yes, I know, but all this—this attention, the ceremonies, this whole Saint Nicolas thing is because of you. It was all your idea. You're the one who should be getting all this attention, not me."

"Well you seem to be doing a fine job for all of us," Harry grinned.

Brookins smiled. "Well in that case, I should get over to the head table, but we've got a lot of catching up to do later."

"I'll be here," Harry said, "Now go on, St. Nick. Do your thing."

Following dinner, several members of the Oeuvre Saint Nicolas delivered tributes to Brookins, Stutz, McClelland and the other men of the 28th Infantry Division's Signal Company Message Center. Then it was time for everyone to mingle and meet the American Saint Nicolas. One by one, everyone in the room stepped up to meet Brookins. They would shake his hand and tell him what an honor it was to meet him, and Brookins would politely listen to their stories and recollections; what the American Saint Nicolas meant to them and their children or how they never forgot what he and the other soldiers did for them throughout the war.

After most of the people had met and talked with Brookins, a member of the NBC camera crew asked if they could have a few minutes to interview him. Brookins, who by now was reveling in the festivities, was more than happy to accommodate, but as he followed the reporter over to where the crew had set up the lights and camera, a man and two middle-aged women stopped him.

"Excuse me, Mister Brookins," the man began. "These women would like to meet you, but they do not speak English."

"Certainly," Brookins said smiling at the already beaming women.

"I can interpret for them," the man added.

One of the women spoke in French, and as the interpreter listened carefully Brookins smiled and nodded, awaiting the translation.

"She says you probably do not remember her," the man related.

"I'm sorry, I don't," Brookins said. "Were you here in 1944?"

The interpreter thought for a moment, and then spoke to the women. The two women looked at each other with surprise and laughed. The second woman spoke to the translator, but before the man could respond, Brookins had pieced together bits of the conversation and a look of surprise spread across his face.

"My angels!" he blurted out with a smile.

No translation was necessary as Brookins and the two women, Liliane Wampach and Jeanny Schleimer exchanged hugs and kisses and tears.

"These were my angels," Brookins said to the interpreter. "I can't believe it! It's so good to see you again," he said hugging them both.

"I remember," Liliane recalled through the interpreter, "The word went around town that the Americans were collecting all their rations to give a party for the children. Then the Mother Superior came into our class to tell us about the party and that two of us would be chosen to be Saint Nicolas' angels."

"Yes, it was such an honor to be chosen," Jeanny said. "I remember you lifting us into the jeep, and we drove through the whole town. Then we went back to the castle for the party."

"Yes, and there was hot cocoa," Liliane continued through the interpreter. "And everyone sang songs. It was such a wonderful day. Then when we were ready to go home, Saint Nicolas came over to us angels and gave each of us a kiss."

Brookins smiled as he recalled the moments the women were talking about.

"Well, I can remember that I tried to talk to you both all day and you didn't say a word. I'm glad you decided to talk to me now," he joked. "I don't suppose you'd want to be my angels again tomorrow?" he teased.

The women laughed, hearing the translation and shaking their heads.

The thought occurred to Brookins that, like the other children in 1944, Liliane and Jeanny had seen him not as a soldier, but as the real Saint Nicolas. What a delight it must have been from a child's perspective, to be Saint Nicolas' helpers and to have him treat them in such a special manner.

"I have to go over there to talk to the camera crew," Brookins explained to the women. "Will you wait here until I'm done?"

The women nodded, and once more, the three of them exchanged hugs. Then Brookins walked over to where the camera crew had set up the lights.

"I know you want to get back to the festivities, so we'll make this as quick as possible," the crew's producer promised as Brookins sat down.

"That's all right," Brookins said as a technician placed a microphone in front of him, "Ask whatever you want. I'm just happy to be here for all of this."

"Let's get started then," the producer said.

As the camera rolled, the producer asked Brookins to describe what it was like the day the Germans retook the town of Wiltz. Brookins thought for a moment and then explained how the attack had caught the Americans by surprise and how he and the other soldiers felt ashamed at being forced to retreat and abandon the people they had come to know so well. To make matters worse, the men had learned that some of the people at the party had been killed and the town of Wiltz destroyed in the fighting that followed the assault.

The producer nodded and asked Brookins if part of the reason he came back was to make amends with the people of Wiltz. After thinking about the question for a moment, Brookins shook his head and explained that he wanted to come back to Wiltz because he felt grateful to the people. They had such tremendous loyalty to American veterans and America in general after all that had happened during the war. He added that he felt proud because in some small way he represented all the men who had helped with the Christmas party, especially those who couldn't be there because they'd lost their lives defending the town.

The cameraman interrupted the producer just as he was preparing to ask another question. "I'll need another reel," he said, quickly swapping out the film.

Brookins' thoughts drifted as he watched the man reload the film. He thought back to the many times he had swapped out reels of film while showing movies to the troops, but before his thoughts could take him too far into the past, the cameraman was ready again.

The producer asked Brookins about the party and what it was like to play Saint Nicolas in 1944. Then he asked if Brookins had been surprised to learn of the town's annual reenactment.

"I sure was!" Brookins exclaimed, "I had no idea that any of this was going on until several months ago when I got a call from Frank McClelland, telling me all about what was happening and that someone from Wiltz would be in touch. You have to remember that it was just one day out of the whole war. Don't get me wrong, it was a wonderful day and we all—that is, the GIs and the kids and everyone—had a great time, but there was still a war going on. We had our jobs to do, and we moved on. We never did come back to Wiltz after the Germans attacked. I had pretty much forgotten about Wiltz and the Christmas party. So when I got the letter from Jeanly Schweig asking me to come back, well, at first I didn't know what to expect. But now, after all this . . . ," Brookins paused as the words began to catch in his throat, "I never knew it meant so much to the people here."

CHAPTER 14

Joseph Scheer was a six-year-old boy in Wiltz when he first met the American Saint Nicolas in 1944. He, like most of the people in Wiltz, had never forgot that day and the generosity of the American soldiers. It was an *event*, a Christmas story, passed down through the generations and retold countless times in homes throughout Wiltz and the surrounding towns. Now forty years old and a father himself, Scheer waited in the cold with his two children and more than three thousand other people to see the American Saint Nicolas once again arrive in Wiltz.

Off in the distance of a clear December sky, the small crowd that had gathered on the outskirts of town could see a helicopter approaching. It was Jeanly Schweig's idea to make the arrival of the American Saint Nicolas, on this thirtieth anniversary, a special one. He contacted the nearby US Army base and persuaded them to join the festivities by flying Brookins into town in one of their helicopters. As the helicopter approached, the rumbling of the engine and the high-pitched thump of the blades grew louder, as did the excitement of the onlookers. They watched as the aircraft gracefully eased its way down from the sky and landed in the middle of an open field. The pilot cut the engine and as the rotor blades stopped turning, one of the doors in the passenger compartment opened. A loud ovation rose from the crowd and echoed through the hills as the unmistakable figure of a man dressed in a gold-trimmed cape and a red bishop's miter, with a puffy white beard and a crosier, emerged from the helicopter. For the first time in more than thirty years, *the* American Saint Nicolas was back in Wiltz.

The mayor of Wiltz, members of the Oeuvre Saint Nicolas, and Father Wolff all greeted Brookins. They exchanged handshakes, and Brookins was ushered over to a parade float built just for the occasion and pulled by a three-quarter-ton battlefield weapon carrier from the war. On the float stood an ornate sleigh adorned with shimmering garlands and flanked on either side by two little girls dressed as angels. Brookins stepped onto the platform, and to the delight of the crowd, started waving. This time, Brookins was well aware of the camera crew filming the event. He waved to the camera and then nodded to the man behind the wheel of the truck hitched to the float. The man gave Saint Nicolas a wave and the float slowly moved forward.

The narrow streets of the town were lined with more people eager to catch a glimpse of the American Saint Nicolas as he made his way to Wiltz Castle and the official ceremony. The route through town was exactly the same as it had been more than thirty years earlier. As the float journeyed through the streets, Brookins waved to the spectators and tried to make eye contact with as many of the children as possible.

"Merry Christmas," he repeated over and over again as he passed out candy to the children, this time tossing it to them from the sleigh.

The ride through town took a bit longer than the Oeuvre Saint Nicolas had planned, but after thirty minutes, the float finally glided up to the Castle's amphitheater, followed by a procession of people from the streets. An anxious crowd waiting at the amphitheater erupted in joyous cheers at the sight of the American Saint Nicolas. An amazed Brookins waved to the crowd for a few moments before stepping down from the float. While a band played and the crowd sang songs in praise of Saint Nicolas, Brookins strode up onto the stage where a group of dignitaries, including Harry Stutz and Frank McClelland, were waiting. When the songs ended and the subsequent applause subsided, Jeanly Schweig walked up to the microphone and addressed the crowd in English.

"What a wonderful day it is here in Wiltz, to have *the* American Saint Nicolas, the very first, Mr. Richard Brookins, here with us to celebrate," Schweig said proudly, and he then paused as the amphitheater once again erupted in applause and cheers.

"We can never forget what these American soldiers did for us and especially for our children."

Another ovation rose from the audience continued for almost a minute. Schweig relished the moment. All the work and fundraising he had done through the years for the various statues and monuments honoring soldiers and their sacrifices paled in the shadow of this, his crowning achievement: bringing *the* American Saint Nicolas back to Wiltz. Schweig raised his hands, quieting the crowd. He cleared his throat and stepped to the microphone.

"It is my pleasure and honor to introduce Mr. Richard Brookins: the American Saint Nicolas."

Everyone in the amphitheater stood, cheering and applauding loudly as the American Saint Nicolas made his way to the podium. Brookins hadn't been nervous about reenacting his role as Saint Nicolas—not when the helicopter approached the landing field and he could see more than a hundred people waiting for his arrival; not when the NBC camera crew began filming, and he knew there was a better-than-average chance that the images caught on film would be seen all over Europe and maybe even in the United States; and not even when the float made its way into the castle courtyard to the delight of more than three thousand people. It wasn't until Brookins began the short walk to the podium that he felt his stomach tighten and his breath quicken. The same anxiety he had felt stepping out of the jeep in 1944 seized him again as he reached the podium and waved to the crowd. He glanced behind him, scanning the faces on the stage until he saw Harry Stutz, who smiled and nodded encouragingly, just as he had thirty years ago. Brookins took a deep breath, and turned back to the crowd, ready to deliver one last surprise for Saint Nicolas Day.

He reached into his pocket and retrieved his notes: words he'd written months ago in anticipation of this moment. Words he sent to Wiltz in a letter. Words that were translated, and then spoken slowly, clearly into a tape recorder and sent back. Words that had been rehearsed for what seemed like a hundred times. With his hand trembling, he adjusted the microphone, and began to speak. The thousands gathered in the amphitheater that day fell silent with astonishment when the American Saint Nicolas spoke not in English or German or French but in Lëtzebuergesch—*their* language once banned.

OF NOTE

n 1944, after returning to Wiltz from Clervaux, Brookins tried unsuccessfully to have Hugh assigned to his unit. A few weeks later in January, during the fighting of "the Bulge," Hugh was captured and spent the rest of the war as a POW. After the war, he returned to Minnesota. Despite their ordeal in Clervaux, Richard and Hugh never saw each other again. Hugh died October 30, 1997 at the age of seventy-two.

Captain Benedict "Ben" Kimmelman stayed behind in Wiltz during the early stages of the "Bulge" to help wounded soldiers and civilians. He fought with courage and distinction while defending the town and was later awarded a silver star. Captured and sent to a POW camp in Eastern Germany, he survived the war and opened a dental practice in Philadelphia, where he often made house calls for people unable to travel. He died in 1999 at the age of eighty-four.

S.Sgt. Henry "Hank" Fiebig survived the war and returned to Empire, Wisconsin, where he married Esther, the love of his life, in 1946. He worked the family farm and continued to play guitar for the next twenty years before moving to Fond Du Lac, where he died on August 29, 1992, at the age of eighty-one.

Tech. Sgt. Harvey Hamann helped cover the divisional withdrawal from Wiltz. He was in the last convoy out of town that was ambushed by the Germans. Forced to scatter into the woods with others in the group, Hamann was captured on December 21, 1944, and was a POW until the end of the war. He settled in the Chicago area, where he married and where he fathered eight children. He died on September 5, 1992, at the age of seventy-three.

Pvt. Keith Burton survived the war and returned the Buffalo, New York, area. He died in March 1978. He was fifty-six.

Jeanly Schweig continued to remember and honor all the soldiers who fought and died to liberate Wiltz by helping organize the Saint Nicolas festivities every year. In 1991, although very ill, Jeanly fulfilled a lifelong wish by finally donning the robes and playing Saint Nicolas for the children of Wiltz. He died four months later on March 11, 1992, at the age of sixty-four.

Father Victor Wolff continued to serve Wiltz and the surrounding communities. In 1986, he celebrated fifty years in the priesthood. He died two years later at the age of seventy-eight.

Cpl. Harry Stutz was also among those who stayed behind to help defend Wiltz during the "Bulge." He, too, was in the last convoy ambushed by Germans on the road to Bastogne. Harry immediately dug a hole on the roadside to bury his wallet, ID card, and dog tags—anything that would identify him as a Jew if captured. However, Harry managed to evade the Germans for the next three days before joining up with other GIs attempting to reach Neufchâteau. Harry Stutz died in Edmonds, Washington, on December 17, 2011, at the age of ninety-four.

Sgt. Frank McClelland was awarded a bronze star for his actions in defending Wiltz during the "Bulge." Frank McClelland died on February 23, 2007, in Dravosburg, Pennsylvania, at the age of ninety-one.

Since their return in 1977, Frank and Harry had each returned to Wiltz several times to visit lifelong friends and take part in the annual Saint Nicolas Day festivities.

Left: Harry Stutz (left) and Richard Brookins (second from right) making a presentation on behalf of the Veterans of the 28th Infantry Division Signal Company Message Center to the City of Wiltz, 1977. *Photo: Richard Brookins*

Above: The American St. Nick arrives in Wiltz, 1977. *Photo: Oeuvre Saint Nicolas, Wiltz*

Below: The American St. Nick parades through Wiltz, 1977. *Photo: Oeuvre Saint Nicolas, Wiltz*

Right: The American St. Nick in Wiltz, 1984.
Photo: Oeuvre St. Nicolas, Wiltz

Below: The American St. Nick in Wiltz, 1984.
Photo: Oeuvre St. Nicolas, Wiltz

Opposite top: Jeanly Schweig, 1988. *Photo: Oeuvre Saint Nicolas, Wiltz*

Opposite bottom: The American St. Nick arrives in Wiltz, 1994. *Photo: Oeuvre Saint Nicolas, Wiltz*

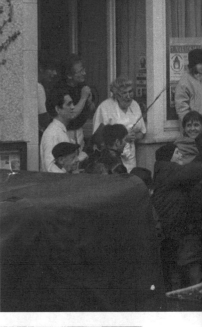

Top left: The American St. Nick at the Wiltz castle, 1994. *Photo: Oeuvre Saint Nicolas, Wiltz*

Top right: The American St. Nick parading through Wiltz, 1999. *Photo: Oeuvre Saint Nicolas, Wiltz*

Bottom left: The American St. Nick flanked by his angels at the Wiltz castle, 1999. *Photo: Oeuvre Saint Nicolas, Wiltz*

Bottom right: The American St. Nick greeting children at the Wiltz castle, 1999. *Photo: Oeuvre Saint Nicolas, Wiltz*

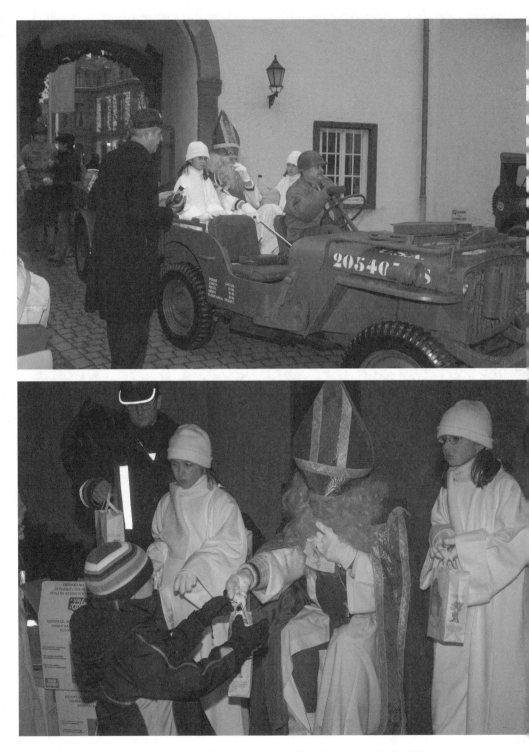

Above: The American St. Nick arriving at the Wiltz castle, 2004. *Photo: Oeuvre Saint Nicolas, Wiltz*

Below: The American St. Nick hands out treats at the Wiltz castle, 2004. *Photo: Oeuvre Saint Nicolas, Wiltz*

Above: Richard Brookins, the American St. Nick, arriving at the Wiltz castle, 2009. *Photo: Oeuvre Saint Nicolas, Wiltz*

Below: The Saint Nicolas festival underway at Wiltz Castle, 2009. *Photo: Oeuvre Saint Nicolas, Wiltz*

Right: Stone memorial to Richard Brookins, the American St. Nick, placed in 2009.

Below: Memorial to the 28th Infantry Division outside the Wiltz castle

1944 – 2009

to Richard Brookins, the American GI of the 28th Infantry Division,
honorary citizen of Wiltz, honorary member of the Oeuvre Saint Nicolas Wiltz
St. Nick for the children of our town, in December 1944

à Richard Brookins, le GI de la 28th Infantry Division,
citoyen d' honneur de Wiltz, membre d' honneur de l' Oeuvre Saint Nicolas
Saint Nicolas pour les enfants de notre ville, en décembre 1944

Le comité de l' Oeuvre Saint Nicolas de Wiltz 28. 11. 2009

Since 1977, Richard Brookins has been invited back to Wiltz every year to re-create his role. He has returned eight times, always marking five-year milestones, including November 2014, when, for the seventieth anniversary of the Saint Nicolas festival, ninety-two-year-old Richard Brookins, *the* American Saint Nicolas, returned to Wiltz one more time.